Recipes for Weight Loss Surgery Success

Also by Chef Dave Fouts

Cookwise
Weight Loss Surgery Cookbook for Dummies

Also by Chef Dave Fouts and Vicki Bovee, MS, RD, LD

Walk from Obesity Cookbook
Ditch Your Diet in 30 Days

Recipes for Weight Loss Surgery Success

Starting Your Journey Step-By-Step

CHEF DAVE FOUTS

AND

VICKI BOVEE, MS, RD, LD

iUniverse, Inc.
Bloomington

Recipes for Weight Loss Surgery Success
Starting Your Journey Step-By-Step

iUniverse books may be ordered through booksellers or by contacting:

iUniverse
1663 Liberty Drive
Bloomington, IN 47403
www.iuniverse.com
1-800-Authors (1-800-288-4677)

ISBN: 978-1-4620-2011-9 (sc)
ISBN: 978-1-4620-2012-6 (ebk)

Printed in the United States of America

iUniverse rev. date: 06/06/2011

SIMPLY
SMART
FOOD INC

Our mission

To help fight the disease of obesity one meal at a time by educating, inspiring, and motivating people to live healthier lives.

Disclaimer

This publication is designed to provide general information regarding the project matter and topics covered herein. The general health and nutritional information provided is intended for informational purposes only. The subject matter is not intended to be a substitute for professional, nutritional, or medical advice, diagnosis, or treatment. Readers of this subject matter should not rely exclusively on the information provided through this subject matter for their own health needs. All specific medically and nutritionally oriented questions should be presented to your own health care provider(s). The nutritional information contained herein should not be considered as comprehensive in nature, and as such, you should consult with your dietitian, surgeon, or healthcare provider to be sure that the recipes and suggestions contained herein are allowed for consumption based on your medical history and your current state of health. If you are unsure of the safety of consuming any of the ingredients listed herein, or whether your medications may be compatible with the ingredients contained herein, you should contact your physician, pharmacist, and/ or healthcare provider.

The authors have taken reasonable precautions in the preparation of this subject matter and facts presented are accurate as of the date written. The subject matter is provided for your reference and is for personal and private use only. The author has attempted to follow all guidelines with regard to The American Society for Metabolic and Bariatric Surgery and the American Dietetic Association. Both the authors and publisher specifically disclaim any liability resulting from the use or application of the information contained in the subject matter. The information contained herein is not intended to serve as medical or nutritional advice, as it relates to an individual's unique situation.

Further, neither the author nor the publisher make any warranties or representations, express or implied as to the accuracy or completeness, timeliness, or usefulness of any option, advice, services, or other information contained or referenced in this subject matter. This cookbook is not to be considered a substitute for nutritional information and no medical information is either provided or implied in any capacity herein.

No part of this publication may be sold or reproduced, stored in a retrieval system, or transmitted in any form or by any means—electronic, mechanical, photocopy, recording, or any other—except for brief credited quotations in printed reviews, without the prior written permission of the authors. The accuracy of the recipes is the responsibility of the original author. The compiler is not responsible for errors. If you purchase this book without a cover, you should be aware that this book might have been stolen property and reported as "unsold and destroyed" to the publisher. In such case, neither the author nor the publisher has received any payment for this "stripped book."

CONTENTS

Introduction

Dear Reader,

Congratulations! You are embarking on an important journey toward a healthier weight and a healthier new life. Your weight loss surgery is a tool that can help you achieve your goals, and we have lots of experience to help you along the way. Chef Dave had gastric bypass surgery in January 2002 and knows firsthand what the journey is like. As a professionally trained chef, he knows how to prepare foods that will work best for you with your new eating plan. Vicki has been working with clients and patients in weight management for more than twenty-five years and has specialized in bariatric nutrition since 2003. We have authored numerous publications regarding healthy cooking, weight management, and bariatric nutrition and have worked with thousands of clients and patients.

We understand that the first few weeks and months after your weight loss surgery can be challenging. The decisions of when to eat, what to eat, and how much to eat are faced daily. We designed the recipes in this book to make those choices easier.

Included are easy recipes to take you from your preoperative weight loss through the diet progression including shakes and smoothies, smooth food, and soft food. All the recipes come from Chef Dave's kitchen so you know they taste good and are easy to prepare. Vicki has analyzed each recipe for nutritional quality using ESHA Research Food Processor SQL Software, Version 10.5 (Salem, OR). Our recommendations follow the guidelines of the American Society for Metabolic and Bariatric

Surgery (ASMBS) and the American Dietetic Association (ADA). Your surgeon or program dietitian will give you recommendations that are more specific in regards to following each step of the diet progression depending on the type of weight loss surgery you have had and your own needs. Always follow the orders from your bariatric health care provider!

Remember that every individual is different. Food tolerances will vary, and we have included foods in our recipes that most people tolerate well. In addition, keep in mind that rate of weight loss varies based on the type of weight loss surgery and the person. Stay focused on your own goals. Try not to compare yourself to others who have had weight loss surgery.

Keep in mind that eating is only a part of your commitment to lifestyle changes. Building a healthier lifestyle includes daily physical activity and dealing with those emotional issues that can lead to overeating. Your weight loss surgery is a tremendous tool, but it cannot work alone. You are the one who will do the work to become successful.

In the upcoming weeks and months, you will start to feel better and have more energy. It is an exciting time. Enjoy the trip!

Warmest regards,

Chef Dave and Vicki

SHAKES AND SMOOTHIES

A Note from Vicki

Protein shakes and smoothies are a great meal or snack whether you are in the preoperative stage of weight loss surgery or months past your surgery. This section of the book is divided into two parts:

> *Protein Supplement Shakes.* These recipes use a powdered protein shake mix with the addition of zero or minimal calorie flavorings. Both preoperative and postoperative patients can use the recipes. Shake mix powders vary greatly in the amount of calories and nutrients per scoop depending on the brand. Check the label of the shake mix you are using and make your shake using the recommended amount.

> Your surgeon may have recommended you lose weight before your surgery by following a mostly liquid diet. There are many shake mixes to choose from and your surgical practice may have specific recommendations. The length of time you will need to be on a liquid diet is determined by your surgeon so be sure to follow the instructions you are given.

> *Smoothies.* These recipes are designed to be used after weight loss surgery and can be used during the smooth food step or for a lifetime. We have developed recipes that do not include protein powder supplements but

do have added calories with the addition of fruit or flavorings.

Protein shakes and smoothies are a great way to help you meet your daily protein requirements, especially in the first weeks or months after surgery. Typically, protein goals are 60 to 100 grams a day after surgery and your program dietitian can provide you with your specific recommendation. It may take you a few weeks or months to meet this protein goal with eating only solid foods because your pouch cannot hold much food at a meal. Protein shakes can increase your protein intake until you can meet the requirements with solid foods.

A protein shake or smoothie can help you meet your daily fluid requirements of a minimum 64 fluid ounces (2 L) per day. Sip, sip, sip! Drinking too fast can cause belching, nausea, discomfort, or regurgitation.

If you are a few days or weeks out from your weight loss surgery you may find it is difficult to drink a protein shake, because you "can't get it past your nose." Occasionally, people notice their sense of smell kicks into high gear after surgery and the smell of the powdered protein may be a problem for you. Drink your shake from a covered cup or glass. This way your nose won't be in the drink! No straws. Drinking through a straw can cause you to suck up too much air into your pouch and cause discomfort.

Protein Supplement Powders

Sometimes choosing a protein shake can be confusing with so many choices on the shelves. Let's look at some of the types of protein most often used for protein shake supplements.

Milk proteins:
- Whey powder comes from taking the whey, the liquid portion, out of the milk during cheese production. The fat is removed and the whey is dried.
- Whey protein concentrate is filtered whey that takes out most of the lactose. Most products are at least 80 percent protein.
- Whey protein isolates are about 90 percent protein concentrate. More lactose and fat is removed than from whey protein concentrate. People who are lactose intolerant can usually use this type of protein without side effects.
- Casein is the major protein found in milk. It is absorbed more slowly than whey.
- Hydrolyzed proteins are broken down into smaller protein chains, which make them easier to digest, and they are more easily absorbed.

Soy protein:
- Soy protein isolate is made from defatted soy meal. Most of the fat and carbohydrates are removed. Most products are 90 percent protein. These are a great choice if you are vegetarian or have milk allergies.

Avoid:
- Collagen based protein powders or drinks. This type of protein is not well absorbed. Switch to a whey protein isolate or soy protein isolate product.

We recommend a protein supplement shake mix that has:
- ✓ 10 grams or more of protein per 100 calories
- ✓ 3 grams of fat or less per 100 calories
- ✓ Less than 12 grams of sugar per serving

Liquids for Mixing

Powdered shake mixes can be made with cold water, fat free or 1 % milk, low lactose milk, or calcium fortified soy milk. If you are mixing the protein powder with milk or soy milk, remember to add the grams of protein from the milk beverage to the total protein grams for your shake.

Rice milk and almond milk can be used, but unless fortified, neither are a good source of protein and calcium. Check the nutrition facts label.

If you are looking for a new shake flavor or want to get back on track, try one of our recipes. They taste good, are easy to prepare, make a great on-the-go food, and are good for you!

Eat Smart . . .

Vicki Bovee, MS, RD, LD

A Note from Chef Dave

A blender is necessary when making the perfect smoothie. A blender combines your shake in a way no other piece of kitchen equipment can. The blades of a blender are shaped like an *X* with the tips pointed down. This configuration allows the blades to chop up the ice while mixing in the remaining ingredients. The tornado-like movement allows the ice and other ingredients to flow to the center, mix and chop, and push the mixed shake to the outside.

Do not expect a food processor or a handheld blender to perform as well as a blender. The blades are different. A food processor has two, *S*-shaped blades spaced over each other. The blades won't catch the ice as well as a blender can and will leave large pieces of ice that won't blend in. As for the handheld blender, most ice cubes used are too large to be effective in the blending process.

The size of the ice used makes the difference between a smoothie and a smoothie "on the rocks." Large cubes of ice wear down the blades of your blender and never completely chop the ice. The best ice cube for the job is a medium cube no larger than ¾-inch. This will allow the blender to grind the ice leaving a smoothie masterpiece.

Placing smoothie ingredients in the proper order into the blender is a vital step for a perfectly mixed smoothie. First, place the water into your blender, add your protein powder and flavorings, and blend. Lastly add the ice and continue blending. This order will keep the dry powder from caking at the bottom of the blender.

Only blend your shakes until creamy. If you blend too long, your shakes will be frothy, foamy, and just plain awful. We have tested these recipes and blend times so they will come close to your home kitchen blender times. If you have a commercial-type blender such as a Vita-Mix or a Magic Bullet, your blend time will be less than the time recommended in the recipes. Remember, we are making shakes and smoothies, not frothies and foamies!

Cook Smart . . .

Chef Dave Fouts

Shakes

Chocolate Mint

Serves 1

1 to 2 scoops chocolate flavored protein powder*
½ cup (125 mL) cold water
1 tsp (5 mL) sugar free chocolate pudding
¼ tsp (1 mL) mint extract
1 cup (250 mL) ice

Directions:
1. Put cold water into blender.
2. Add protein powder, sugar free chocolate pudding, and mint extract.
3. Place lid on top of blender and blend for 15 to 20 seconds.
4. Add ice and blend for 30 to 45 seconds.
5. Serve chilled.

Follow recommended scoops per serving size on container.

Nutritional value will depend on protein supplement powder used. Added ingredients contribute minimal calories or nutritive value to your shake.

Chocoholic

Serves 1

1 to 2 scoops chocolate flavored protein powder*
½ cup (125 mL) cold water
1 tsp (5 mL) sugar free chocolate syrup
¼ tsp (1 mL) butter extract
1 cup (250 mL) ice

Directions:
1. Put cold water into blender.
2. Add protein powder, sugar free chocolate syrup, and butter extract.
3. Place lid on top of blender and blend for 15 to 20 seconds.
4. Add ice and blend for 30 to 45 seconds.
5. Serve chilled.

Follow recommended scoops per serving size on container.

Nutritional value will depend on protein supplement powder used. Added ingredients contribute minimal calories or nutritive value to your shake.

Lemon Chiffon

Serves 1

1 to 2 scoops vanilla flavored protein powder*
½ cup (125 mL) cold water
¼ tsp (1 mL) sugar free lemon gelatin powder
1 tsp (5 mL) sugar free lemon pudding powder
⅛ tsp vanilla extract
1 cup (250 mL) ice

Directions:
1. Put cold water into blender.
2. Add protein powder, sugar free lemon gelatin, lemon pudding, and vanilla extract.
3. Place lid on top of blender and blend for 15 to 20 seconds.
4. Add ice and blend for 30 to 45 seconds.
5. Serve chilled.

Follow recommended scoops per serving size on container.

Nutritional value will depend on protein supplement powder used. Added ingredients contribute minimal calories or nutritive value to your shake.

Limealicious

Serves 1

1 to 2 scoops vanilla flavored protein powder*
½ cup (125 mL) cold water
¼ tsp (1 mL) sugar free lime gelatin powder
⅛ tsp vanilla extract
1 cup (250 mL) ice

Directions:
1. Put cold water into blender.
2. Add protein powder, sugar free lime gelatin, and vanilla extract.
3. Place lid on top of blender and blend for 15 to 20 seconds.
4. Add ice and blend for 30 to 45 seconds.
5. Serve chilled.

Follow recommended scoops per serving size on container.

Nutritional value will depend on protein supplement powder used. Added ingredients contribute no calories or nutritive value to your shake.

Mocha Frappuccino

Serves 1

1 to 2 scoops chocolate flavored protein powder*
½ cup (125 mL) cold water
1 tsp (5 mL) sugar free chocolate syrup
1 tsp (5 mL) decaffeinated instant coffee
1 cup (250 mL) ice

Directions:
1. Put cold water into blender.
2. Add protein powder, sugar free chocolate syrup, and instant decaf coffee.
3. Place lid on top of blender and blend for 15 to 20 seconds.
4. Add ice and blend for 30 to 45 seconds.
5. Serve chilled.

Follow recommended scoops per serving size on container.

Nutritional value will depend on protein supplement powder used. Added ingredients contribute minimal calories or nutritive value to your shake.

Orange Creamcicle

Serves 1

1 to 2 scoops vanilla flavored protein powder*
½ cup (125 mL) cold water
¼ tsp (1 mL) sugar free orange gelatin powder
⅛ tsp vanilla extract
1 cup (250 mL) ice

Directions:
1. Put cold water into blender.
2. Add protein powder, sugar free orange gelatin, and vanilla extract.
3. Place lid on top of blender and blend for 15 to 20 seconds.
4. Add ice and blend for 30 to 45 seconds.
5. Serve chilled.

Follow recommended scoops per serving size on container.

Nutritional value will depend on protein supplement powder used. Added ingredients contribute no calories or nutritive value to your shake.

Smooth Banana

Serves 1

1 to 2 scoops vanilla flavored protein powder*
½ cup (125 mL) cold water
1 tsp (5 mL) sugar free banana pudding powder
⅛ tsp butter extract
1 cup (250 mL) ice

Directions:
1. Put cold water into blender first.
2. Add protein powder, sugar free banana pudding, and butter extract.
3. Place lid on top of blender and blend for 15 to 20 seconds.
4. Add ice and blend for 30 to 45 seconds.
5. Serve chilled.

Follow recommended scoops per serving size on container.

Nutritional value will depend on protein supplement powder used. Added ingredients contribute minimal calories or nutritive value to your shake.

Strawberry Chocolate Perfection

Serves 1

1 to 2 scoops chocolate flavored protein powder*
½ cup (125 mL) cold water
1 tsp (5 mL) sugar free strawberry gelatin powder
⅛ tsp vanilla extract
1 cup (250 mL) ice

Directions:
1. Put cold water into blender.
2. Add protein powder, sugar free strawberry gelatin, and vanilla extract.
3. Place lid on top of blender and blend for 15 to 20 seconds.
4. Add ice and blend for 30 to 45 seconds.
5. Serve chilled.

Follow recommended scoops per serving size on container.

Nutritional value will depend on protein supplement powder used. Added ingredients contribute no calories or nutritive value to your shake.

Vanilla Cherry Delight

Serves 1

1 to 2 scoops vanilla flavored protein powder*
½ cup (125 mL) cold water
¼ tsp (1 mL) sugar free cherry gelatin powder
⅛ tsp vanilla extract
1 cup (250 mL) ice

Directions:
1. Put cold water into blender.
2. Add protein powder, sugar free cherry gelatin, and vanilla extract.
3. Place lid on top of blender and blend for 15 to 20 seconds.
4. Add ice and blend for 30 to 45 seconds.
5. Serve chilled.

Follow recommended scoops per serving size on container.

Nutritional value will depend on protein supplement powder used. Added ingredients contribute no calories or nutritive value to your shake.

Very Vanilla Yum

Serves 1

1 to 2 scoops vanilla flavored protein powder*
½ cup (125 mL) cold water
¼ tsp (1 mL) sugar free vanilla pudding powder
⅛ tsp vanilla extract
1 cup (250 mL) ice

Directions:
1. Put cold water into blender.
2. Add protein powder, sugar free vanilla pudding powder, and vanilla extract.
3. Place lid on top of blender and blend for 15 to 20 seconds.
4. Add ice and blend for 30 to 45 seconds.
5. Serve chilled.

Follow recommended scoops per serving size on container.

Nutritional value will depend on protein supplement powder used. Added ingredients contribute minimal calories or nutritive value to your shake.

Smoothies

Banana Berry

Serves 1

½ cup (125 mL) fat free milk
2 tbsp (30 mL) nonfat dry powdered milk
¼ cup (50 mL) blueberries
¼ cup (50 mL) raspberries
¼ cup (50 mL) sliced bananas
⅛ tsp vanilla extract
1 packet sugar substitute or to taste
¼ cup (50 mL) ice

Directions:
1. Stir the powdered milk into the fat free milk and let stand for 2 to 3 minutes.
2. Place all ingredients into blender and blend for 1 to 2 minutes or until well blended.
3. Serve chilled.

Nutrition Facts	Amount		Amount	
Serves 1	**Fat**	0 g	**Carbohydrate**	29 g
Serving size 1½ cup (375 mL)	Saturated Fat	0 g	Fiber	2 g
Calories 140	**Cholesterol**	5 mg	Sugar	19 g
Calories from Fat 5	**Sodium**	100 mg	**Protein**	8 g
% Daily Value Vitamin A 10%	Vitamin C 20%	Calcium 30%	Iron 2%	

Chocolate-Covered Berries

Serves 1

¼ cup (50 mL) fat free milk
2 tbsp (30 mL) nonfat dry powdered milk
¼ cup (50 mL) raspberries
¼ cup (50 mL) sliced strawberries
¼ cup (50 mL) plain nonfat yogurt
1 tbsp (15 mL) sugar free chocolate syrup
1 packet sugar substitute or to taste
¼ cup (50 mL) ice

Directions:
1. Stir the powdered milk into the fat free milk and let stand for 2 to 3 minutes.
2. Place all ingredients into blender and blend for 1 to 2 minutes or until well blended.
3. Serve chilled.

Nutrition Facts	Amount		Amount	
Serves 1	**Fat**	0 g	**Carbohydrate**	22 g
Serving size 1½ cup (375 mL)	Saturated Fat	0 g	Fiber	1 g
Calories 110	**Cholesterol**	5 mg	Sugar	13 g
Calories from Fat 0	**Sodium**	170 mg	**Protein**	8 g
% Daily Value Vitamin A 10%	Vitamin C 60%	Calcium 30%	Iron 4%	

Mango Twister

Serves 1

¼ cup (50 mL) calcium fortified plain soy milk
2 tbsp (30 mL) nonfat dry powdered milk
½ cup (125 mL) fresh mango, peeled, seeded, and chopped
¼ cup (50 mL) orange juice
1 packet sugar substitute or to taste
¼ cup (50 mL) ice

Directions:
1. Stir the powdered milk into the plain soy milk and let stand for 2 to 3 minutes.
2. Place all ingredients into blender and blend for 1 to 2 minutes or until well blended.
3. Serve chilled.

Nutrition Facts	Amount		Amount	
Serves 1	Fat	1 g	Carbohydrate	29 g
Serving size 1½ cup (375 mL)	Saturated Fat	0 g	Fiber	2 g
Calories 140	Cholesterol	0 mg	Sugar	19 g
Calories from Fat 10	Sodium	70 mg	Protein	5 g
% Daily Value Vitamin A 20%	Vitamin C 80%	Calcium 15%	Iron 2%	

Peanut Butter and Banana

Serves 1

1 tbsp (15 mL) creamy natural peanut butter
¼ cup (50 mL) sliced bananas
¼ cup (50 mL) calcium fortified plain soy milk
½ cup (125 mL) plain nonfat yogurt
1 packet sugar substitute or to taste
¼ cup (50 mL) ice

Directions:
1. Place all ingredients into blender and blend for 1 to 2 minutes or until well blended.
2. Serve chilled.

Nutrition Facts	Amount		Amount	
Serves 1	**Fat**	9 g	**Carbohydrate**	26 g
Serving size 1½ cup (375 mL)	Saturated Fat	1 g	Fiber	2 g
Calories 210	**Cholesterol**	5 mg	Sugar	15 g
Calories from Fat 80	**Sodium**	150 mg	**Protein**	10 g
% Daily Value Vitamin A 10%	Vitamin C 15%	Calcium 15%	Iron 2%	

Pineapple Lush

Serves 1

¼ cup (50 mL) canned, crushed pineapple in its own juice, drained
¼ cup (50 mL) silken soft tofu
¼ cup (50 mL) fat free milk
¼ tsp (1 mL) coconut extract
1 packet sugar substitute or to taste
¼ cup (50 mL) ice

Directions:

1. Place all ingredients into blender and blend for 1 to 2 minutes or until well blended.
2. Serve chilled.

Nutrition Facts	Amount		Amount	
Serves 1	**Fat**	1 g	**Carbohydrate**	11 g
Serving size 1 cup (250 mL)	Saturated Fat	0 g	Fiber	1 g
Calories 70	**Cholesterol**	0 mg	Sugar	10 g
Calories from Fat 10	**Sodium**	25 mg	**Protein**	5 g

% Daily Value   Vitamin A 2%   Vitamin C 8%   Calcium 10%   Iron 4%

Pumpkin Spice

Serves 1

2 tbsp (30 mL) canned pumpkin pulp
½ cup (125 mL) silken soft tofu
¼ cup (50 mL) plain nonfat yogurt
¼ cup (50 mL) fat free milk
¼ tsp (1 mL) pumpkin pie spice
⅛ tsp butter extract
2 packets sugar substitute or to taste
¼ cup (50 mL) ice

Directions:
1. Place all ingredients into blender and blend for 1 to 2 minutes or until well blended.
2. Serve chilled.

Nutrition Facts	Amount		Amount	
Serves 1	**Fat**	3 g	**Carbohydrate**	12 g
Serving size 1½ cup (375 mL)	Saturated Fat	0 g	Fiber	2 g
Calories 110	**Cholesterol**	0 mg	Sugar	7 g
Calories from Fat 25	**Sodium**	60 mg	**Protein**	10 g
% Daily Value Vitamin A 90%	Vitamin C 6%	Calcium 25%	Iron 6%	

Spiced Pear

Serves 1

½ cup (125 mL) peeled and cored pear, cut into small pieces
½ cup (125 mL) plain nonfat yogurt
¼ cup (50 mL) fat free milk
¼ tsp (1 mL) pumpkin pie spice
⅛ tsp butter extract
¼ cup (50 mL) ice

Directions:
1. Place all ingredients into blender and blend for 1 to 2 minutes or until well blended.
2. Serve chilled.

Nutrition Facts	Amount		Amount	
Serves 1	**Fat**	0 g	**Carbohydrate**	25 g
Serving size 1½ cup (375 mL)	Saturated Fat	0 g	Fiber	2 g
Calories 120	**Cholesterol**	5 mg	Sugar	17 g
Calories from Fat 0	**Sodium**	95 mg	**Protein**	7 g
% Daily Value Vitamin A 15%	Vitamin C 15%	Calcium 25%	Iron 0%	

Strawberries and Cream

Serves 1

¼ cup (50 mL) fat free milk
2 tbsp (30 mL) nonfat dry powdered milk
¼ cup (50 mL) plain nonfat yogurt
½ cup (125 mL) sliced strawberries
¼ tsp (1 mL) vanilla extract
1 packet sugar substitute or to taste
¼ cup (50 mL) ice

Directions:
1. Stir the powdered milk into the fat free milk and let stand for 2 to 3 minutes.
2. Place all ingredients into blender and blend for 1 to 2 minutes or until well blended.
3. Serve chilled.

Nutrition Facts	Amount		Amount	
Serves 1	**Fat**	0 g	**Carbohydrate**	19 g
Serving size 1½ cup (375 mL)	Saturated Fat	0 g	Fiber	2 g
Calories 110	**Cholesterol**	5 mg	Sugar	15 g
Calories from Fat 5	**Sodium**	110 mg	**Protein**	8 g
% Daily Value Vitamin A 10%	Vitamin C 90%	Calcium 30%	Iron 2%	

Strawberry Cheesecake

Serves 1

½ cup (125 mL) sliced fresh strawberries
¼ cup (50 mL) part skim ricotta cheese
½ cup (125 mL) fat free milk
¼ tsp (1 mL) lemon extract.
1 packet sugar substitute or to taste
¼ cup (50 mL) ice

Directions:
1. Place all ingredients into blender and blend for 1 to 2 minutes or until well blended.
2. Serve chilled.

Nutrition Facts	Amount		Amount	
Serves 1	**Fat**	5 g	**Carbohydrate**	16 g
Serving size 1½ cup (375 mL)	Saturated Fat	3 g	Fiber	2 g
Calories 160	**Cholesterol**	20 mg	Sugar	10 g
Calories from Fat 5	**Sodium**	130 mg	**Protein**	12 g

% Daily Value   Vitamin A 10%   Vitamin C 80%   Calcium 35%   Iron 4%

Sweet Peaches

Serves 1

¼ cup (50 mL) calcium fortified plain soy milk
2 tbsp (30 mL) nonfat dry powdered milk
¼ cup (50 mL) plain nonfat yogurt
¼ cup (50 mL) peaches in light syrup, drained
⅛ tsp butter extract
1 packet sugar substitute or to taste
¼ cup (50 mL) ice

Directions:
1. Stir the powdered milk into the soy milk and let stand for 2 to 3 minutes.
2. Place all ingredients into blender and blend for 1 to 2 minutes or until well blended.
3. Serve chilled.

Nutrition Facts	Amount		Amount	
Serves 1	**Fat**	1 g	**Carbohydrate**	22 g
Serving size 1½ cup (375 mL)	Saturated Fat	0 g	Fiber	1 g
Calories 120	**Cholesterol**	0 mg	Sugar	16 g
Calories from Fat 10	**Sodium**	115 mg	**Protein**	8 g
% Daily Value Vitamin A 15%	Vitamin C 8%	Calcium 20%	Iron 2%	

SMOOTH FOODS

A Note from Vicki

After weight loss surgery, your new pouch needs time to heal. There will be swelling inside of you, so you will need to follow the progressive diet steps to prevent problems with staple lines and/or sutures. Smooth food, or pureed food, is usually the third step of your diet progression after clear and full liquids. Smooth foods are foods that have been put through the food processor to remove the lumps and bumps. Your foods should be of dip consistency or the consistency of applesauce. You don't want any food getting stuck trying to pass through your band or the small opening from your pouch! Having food stuck causes discomfort and pain. It also increases the risk of vomiting, which can put stress on your staple and/or suture lines. Your surgeon or dietitian will recommend you start smooth foods usually 1 to 3 weeks after surgery and follow this diet for 1 to 4 weeks. Always follow the recommendations given to you by your bariatric team.

If you have had adjustable gastric banding, it pays to become familiar with this stage of the diet progression. After you have a fill, or an adjustment to your band, you will need to eat smooth foods for 1 to 2 days after the fill.

Your portions will be very small and based on volume, such as ¼ cup (50 mL), not weight. Using standardized measuring cups and measuring spoons will help you determine the right amount of food. It is important that you do not overfill your new pouch as this can cause discomfort.

A lifetime goal after weight loss surgery is to eat to the point of being no longer hungry. This a skill that is learned by practice, so pay attention to your pouch even in the early days after surgery.

The desire to eat may be present in the absence of hunger. Remember that hunger and the desire to eat are not the same thing, and it takes time for your head to get in touch with your pouch. Typically, when people yield to the desire to eat during this step, they are choosing foods that are too solid for the pouch to tolerate.

Something to keep in mind is to add new foods one at a time. If you have difficulty tolerating a food, it is easier to figure out which one is the troublemaker if you have added only one new food rather than several.

Because your portions are limited, it will be difficult for you to meet your nutritional needs. Remember to eat protein foods first and to eat 4 to 6 times a day during the smooth-food step. Take small bites and eat slowly. Do not drink beverages during your meal, and wait 30 to 60 minutes after your meal before drinking beverages.

We know you can be anxious to move onto solid foods sooner than is recommended by your surgeon or dietitian, but it is best to avoid this temptation. Eating solid foods too soon can create discomfort, pain, and/or regurgitation. We hope we have made this step of your diet progression easier and tastier!

Eat Smart . . .

Vicki Bovee, MS, RD, LD

A Note from Chef Dave

After undergoing weight loss surgery myself in 2002, the dreaded puree, mushy diet was weighing heavy on my mind, no pun intended. I understood the reason for this necessary step in the progression of eating, but as a chef, I knew there had to be a better way. The first task was removing the negative connotation of pureed food. By calling this step "Smooth Foods," it helped make the food more appealing. The second task was making sure that the food had some texture. Smooth food, with the consistency of a dip or a spread, has turned this dreaded step into an acceptable, and yes, a great tasting step on your weight loss journey.

These recipes have been developed and tested in my own kitchen. Each recipe has flavor and texture to help you through the essential step of smooth food. The food processor may not break down the foods if you change the recipe, so please prepare the recipes as I have created them.

You will need to use a food processor, not a blender. A food processor minces, purees, and chops food. A blender mixes drinks and purees liquid. If you were to try to puree food in a blender, it would require more liquid to get the blades in the blender rotating, and you would end up with a fish shake, not a fish dip. A food processor keeps the food moving with little moisture needed.

We recommend a mini food chopper for making your smooth foods. The bowl is smaller and works better for small amounts of food.

I'm often asked about freezing smooth foods. Yes, you can freeze these foods in ice cube trays. It's easy to do and can save you time and money.

1. Make sure your ice cube tray is clean and wiped dry.
2. Spray your ice cube tray with a nonstick cooking spray.
3. Place your prepared smooth food into each cube of the tray, leaving ¼ -inch from the top to allow for expansion.
4. Wrap the filled ice cube tray with plastic wrap and freeze.
5. When the food is frozen, remove the food cubes from the tray and place into airtight containers.
6. To heat, simply remove 1 to 2 cubes from the tray and heat in a microwave until heated through.

For a standard ice cube tray, each cube yields about 2 tablespoons (30 mL) of food.

A final note about using commercial baby food. Baby food is too thin. Smooth foods should have texture and be thicker than ketchup. Baby food is the opposite. Most baby foods can be sipped through a straw. This is excessively thin and can cause you to be hungrier sooner because your pouch will empty more quickly. Baby food also has very little flavor and no texture.

Cook Smart . . .

Chef Dave Fouts

Smooth Food Breakfasts

Apple Delight Malt-O-Meal

Serves 3
Serving size: ¼ cup (50 mL)

¼ cup (50 mL) fat free, 1 %, or calcium fortified soy milk
½ cup (125 mL) unsweetened applesauce
3 tablespoons (45 mL) unflavored Malt-o-Meal
1 packet sugar substitute

Directions:
1. Mix milk and applesauce together; add Malt-o-Meal.
2. Cook according to package directions.
3. Add sugar substitute and mix well.

Flavor ideas: Use ¼ tsp (1 mL) strawberry extract, vanilla extract, or almond extract.

Nutrition Facts	Amount		Amount	
Serves 3	**Fat**	0.5 g	**Carbohydrate**	15 g
Serving size ¼ cup (50 mL)	Saturated Fat	0 g	Fiber	1 g
Calories 70	**Cholesterol**	0 mg	Sugar	5 g
Calories from Fat 0	**Sodium**	10 mg	**Protein**	2 g
% Daily Value Vitamin A 2%	Vitamin C 0%	Calcium 6%	Iron 20%	

Butter Almond Oatmeal

Serves 3
Serving size: ¼ cup (50 mL)

3 tbsp quick cooking oats (45 mL) *or* 1 package plain instant oatmeal
⅔ cup (150 mL) fat free, 1 %, or calcium fortified soy milk
¼ tsp (5 mL) butter extract
Dash almond extract
1 packet sugar substitute

Directions:
1. Cook oats with milk following package directions.
2. Place all ingredients into mini food chopper and blend until smooth.

Nutrition Facts	Amount		Amount	
Serves 3	**Fat**	0 g	**Carbohydrate**	8 g
Serving size ¼ cup (50 mL)	Saturated Fat	0 g	Fiber	0 g
Calories 50	**Cholesterol**	5 mg	Sugar	4 g
Calories from Fat 5	**Sodium**	40 mg	**Protein**	4 g

% Daily Value   Vitamin A 4%   Vitamin C 0%   Calcium 10%   Iron 2%

Cream of Banana

Serves 3
Serving size: ¼ cup (50 mL)

½ cup (125 mL) sliced bananas
¼ cup (50 mL) part skim ricotta cheese
1 packet sugar substitute
¼ tsp (1 mL) vanilla extract

Directions:
1. Place all ingredients into a mini food chopper and blend until smooth.

Nutrition Facts	Amount		Amount	
Serves 3	**Fat**	1.5 g	**Carbohydrate**	7 g
Serving size ¼ cup (50 mL)	Saturated Fat	1 g	Fiber	1 g
Calories 50	**Cholesterol**	5 mg	Sugar	13 g
Calories from Fat 15	**Sodium**	25 mg	**Protein**	3 g
% Daily Value Vitamin A 2%	Vitamin C 4%	Calcium 6%	Iron 0%	

Creamy Scrambled Egg

Serves 1
Serving size: ¼ cup (50 mL)

1 large egg
1 tsp (5 mL) 1 % milk
½ tsp (2 mL) butter
1 slice 2 % milk American cheese, cut into small pieces

Directions:
1. In a small bowl whisk together egg and milk until smooth.
2. In a small sauté pan, melt butter over medium heat.
3. When butter is melted, pour egg mixture into pan.
4. Add cheese and mix until cheese has melted and eggs become light and soft, approximately 3 to 4 minutes cook time.

Nutrition Facts	Amount		Amount	
Serves 1	Fat	9 g	Carbohydrate	3 g
Serving size ¼ cup (50 mL)	Saturated Fat	4 g	Fiber	0 g
Calories 140	**Cholesterol**	195 mg	Sugar	3 g
Calories from Fat 80	**Sodium**	350 mg	**Protein**	10 g
% Daily Value Vitamin A 10%	Vitamin C 0%	Calcium 25%	Iron 6%	

Greek Lemon Yogurt

Serves 1
Serving size: ¼ cup (50 mL)

¼ cup (50 mL) plain Greek nonfat yogurt
Dash lemon extract
1 packet sugar substitute

Directions:
1. Place all ingredients into a bowl and blend until smooth.

Flavor ideas: Use a dash of vanilla or almond extract.

Nutrition Facts	Amount		Amount	
Serves 1	**Fat**	0 g	**Carbohydrate**	3 g
Serving size ¼ cup (50 mL)	Saturated Fat	0 g	Fiber	0 g
Calories 30	**Cholesterol**	0 mg	Sugar	2 g
Calories from Fat 0	**Sodium**	20 mg	**Protein**	5 g
% Daily Value Vitamin A 0%	Vitamin C 0%	Calcium 4%	Iron 0%	

Ricotta Cheese Pumpkin Custard

Serves 1
Serving size: ¼ cup (50 mL)

¼ cup (50 mL) part skim ricotta cheese
1 tbsp (15 mL) canned pumpkin pulp
¼ tsp (1 mL) pumpkin pie spice
⅛ tsp vanilla extract

Directions:
1. Place ingredients into a small bowl and mix well.

Note: This recipe can be made in a larger amount and stored in an airtight container for up to 3 days.

Nutrition Facts	Amount		Amount	
Serves 1	**Fat**	5 g	**Carbohydrate**	4 g
Serving size ¼ cup (50 mL)	Saturated Fat	3 g	Fiber	1 g
Calories 90	**Cholesterol**	20 mg	Sugar	1 g
Calories from Fat 45	**Sodium**	80 mg	**Protein**	7 g
% Daily Value Vitamin A 50%	Vitamin C 0%	Calcium 15%	Iron 2%	

Smooth Blueberry Yogurt

Serves 3
Serving size: ¼ cup (50 mL)

½ cup (125 mL) plain Greek nonfat yogurt
¼ cup (50 mL) frozen blueberries
¼ cup (50 mL) fat free, 1 %, or calcium fortified soy milk
1 packet sugar substitute

Directions:
1. Place all ingredients into a mini food chopper and blend until smooth.

Nutrition Facts	Amount		Amount	
Serves 3	**Fat**	0 g	**Carbohydrate**	4 g
Serving size ¼ cup (50 mL)	Saturated Fat	0 g	Fiber	0 g
Calories 35	**Cholesterol**	0 mg	Sugar	4 g
Calories from Fat 0	**Sodium**	25 mg	**Protein**	4 g

% Daily Value   Vitamin A 0%   Vitamin C 0%   Calcium 6%   Iron 0%

Spiced Cream of Wheat

Serves 3
Serving size: ¼ cup (50 mL)

3 tbsp (45 mL) unflavored Cream of Wheat *or* 1 packet unflavored Cream of Wheat
¾ cup (175 mL) fat free, 1 %, or calcium fortified soy milk
⅛ tsp pumpkin pie spice
1 packet sugar substitute

Directions:
1. Cook Cream of Wheat with milk following package directions.
2. Add pumpkin pie spice and sugar substitute; mix well.

Flavor ideas: Use lemon, vanilla, or almond extract.

Nutrition Facts	Amount		Amount	
Serves 3	**Fat**	0 g	**Carbohydrate**	9 g
Serving size ¼ cup (50 mL)	Saturated Fat	0 g	Fiber	0 g
Calories 50	**Cholesterol**	0 mg	Sugar	3 g
Calories from Fat 0	**Sodium**	85 mg	**Protein**	3 g
% Daily Value Vitamin A 10%	Vitamin C 0%	Calcium 15%	Iron 15%	

Strawberries and Cottage Cheese

Serves 2
Serving size: ¼ cup (50 mL)

¼ cup (50 mL) sliced strawberries
¼ cup (50 mL) small curd low fat cottage cheese
1 packet sugar substitute

Directions:
1. Place strawberries into a mini food chopper and puree.
2. In small bowl, mix cottage cheese, pureed strawberries, and sugar substitute.

Note: This recipe can be made into a larger amount and stored in an airtight container for up to 3 days.

Nutrition Facts	Amount		Amount	
Serves 2	**Fat**	5 g	**Carbohydrate**	3 g
Serving size ¼ cup (50 mL)	Saturated Fat	0 g	Fiber	0 g
Calories 30	**Cholesterol**	5 mg	Sugar	2 g
Calories from Fat 5	**Sodium**	95 mg	**Protein**	3 g

% Daily Value   Vitamin A 0%   Vitamin C 20%   Calcium 2%   Iron 0%

Yocotta

Serves 2
Serving size: ¼ cup (50 mL)

¼ cup (50 mL) light fruit flavored yogurt
¼ cup (50 mL) part skim ricotta cheese

Directions:
1. Place ingredients into a small bowl and mix well.

Flavor ideas:
Extracts: ¼ tsp (1 mL) vanilla, rum, almond, banana, or coconut.
Spices: ⅛ tsp: cinnamon, nutmeg, or pumpkin pie spices.

Nutrition Facts	Amount		Amount	
Serves 2	Fat	2.5 g	Carbohydrate	4 g
Serving size ¼ cup (50 mL)	Saturated Fat	1.5 g	Fiber	0 g
Calories 60	**Cholesterol**	10 mg	Sugar	2 g
Calories from Fat 20	**Sodium**	60 mg	**Protein**	5 g

% Daily Value   Vitamin A 2%   Vitamin C 0%   Calcium 15%   Iron 0%

Smooth Food Lunches

Albacore Tuna Dip

Serves 3
Serving size: ¼ cup (50 mL)

One 6-oz (170 g) can water-packed albacore tuna, drained
2 tbsp (30 mL) light mayonnaise
1 tbsp (15 mL) fat free sour cream
½ tsp (2 mL) garlic powder
Dash chili powder
½ tsp (2 mL) lime juice

Directions:
1. Place all ingredients into mini food chopper and puree for 20 seconds.
2. Using a rubber spatula, scrape down the sides of the bowl and puree for 20 seconds or until smooth.

Nutrition Facts	Amount		Amount	
Serves 3	**Fat**	3.5 g	**Carbohydrate**	2 g
Serving size ¼ cup (50 mL)	Saturated Fat	0.5 g	Fiber	0 g
Calories 90	**Cholesterol**	25 mg	Sugar	1 g
Calories from Fat 35	**Sodium**	270 mg	**Protein**	10 g
% Daily Value Vitamin A 2%	Vitamin C 0% Calcium 2%		Iron 0%	

Chicken Tacos

Serves 4
Serving size: ¼ cup

1 tsp (5 mL) canola oil
½ lb (225 g) boneless, skinless chicken breast, cut into small cubes
½ tsp (2 mL) taco seasoning
2 tbsp (30 mL) shredded reduced fat sharp cheddar cheese
1 tsp (5 mL) light sour cream
2 tsp (10 mL) mild taco sauce

Directions:
1. In a medium sauté pan, heat oil over medium high heat.
2. Add chicken and taco seasoning; mix. Cook for 5 to 7 minutes or until chicken reaches 165°F (75°C).
3. Place chicken and cheese into mini food chopper and puree for 20 seconds.
4. Using a rubber spatula, scrape down the sides of the bowl and puree for 20 seconds or until smooth.
5. Garnish with sour cream and taco sauce.

Nutrition Facts	Amount		Amount	
Serves 4	**Fat**	3.5 g	**Carbohydrate**	1 g
Serving size ¼ cup (50 mL)	Saturated Fat	1 g	Fiber	0 g
Calories 110	**Cholesterol**	50 mg	Sugar	0 g
Calories from Fat 30	**Sodium**	100 mg	**Protein**	19 g

% Daily Value   Vitamin A 0%   Vitamin C 0%   Calcium 2%   Iron 4%

Crab Louie

Serves 3
Serving size: ¼ cup (50 mL)

6 oz (170 g) cooked crab
1 tsp (5 mL) light mayonnaise
½ tsp (2 mL) lemon juice
1 tbsp (15 mL) chili sauce
1 tbsp (15 mL) chopped tomato
1 tsp (5 mL) chopped green onions
Salt and pepper to taste

Directions:
1. Place all ingredients into mini food chopper and puree for 20 seconds.
2. Using a rubber spatula, scrape the sides of the bowl and puree for 20 seconds or until smooth.

Nutrition Facts	Amount		Amount	
Serves 3	**Fat**	1 g	**Carbohydrate**	1 g
Serving size ¼ cup (50 mL)	Saturated Fat	0 g	Fiber	0 g
Calories 60	**Cholesterol**	50 mg	Sugar	0 g
Calories from Fat 10	**Sodium**	200 mg	**Protein**	12 g

% Daily Value   Vitamin A 2%   Vitamin C 8%   Calcium 6%   Iron 2%

Egg Mexi Melt

Serves 1
Serving size: ¼ cup (50 mL)

1 large egg
1 tsp (5 mL) taco seasoning
1 tbsp (15 mL) shredded reduced fat sharp cheddar cheese
½ tsp (2 mL) butter
1 tsp (5 mL) light sour cream
½ tsp (2 mL) mild taco sauce

Directions:
1. Place egg and taco seasoning into a small mixing bowl and whisk until smooth.
2. Add cheese to egg mixture.
3. In a small sauté pan, melt butter over medium heat.
4. Add egg mixture to pan and cook until soft and fluffy, approximately 2 to 3 minutes.
5. Garnish with sour cream and taco sauce.

Note: To reduce cholesterol, omit egg and use ¼ cup (50 mL) egg substitute.

Nutrition Facts	Amount		Amount	
Serves 1	Fat	7 g	Carbohydrate	4 g
Serving size ¼ cup (50 mL)	Saturated Fat	3 g	Fiber	0 g
Calories 120	**Cholesterol**	190 mg	Sugar	2 g
Calories from Fat 60	**Sodium**	310 mg	**Protein**	8 g

% Daily Value   Vitamin A 8%   Vitamin C 0%   Calcium 6%   Iron 6%

Garlic Cilantro Chicken Salad

Serves 4
Serving size: ¼ cup (50 mL)

One 6-oz (170 g) can chicken breast, drained, reserve 1 tbsp (15 mL) broth
1 ½ tsp (7 mL) light mayonnaise
1 tsp (5 mL) lime juice
½ tsp (2 mL) onion powder
½ tsp (2 mL) garlic powder
¼ tsp (1 mL) chili powder
1 tsp (5 mL) chopped cilantro
Salt and pepper to taste

Directions:
1. Place all ingredients into mini food chopper.
2. Puree for 30 seconds.
3. Using a rubber spatula, scrape down the sides of the bowl.
4. Add more chicken broth if a thinner consistency is desired and blend another 15 seconds.

Nutrition Facts	Amount		Amount	
Serves 4	**Fat**	1.5 g	**Carbohydrate**	1 g
Serving size ¼ cup (50 mL)	Saturated Fat	0 g	Fiber	0 g
Calories 60	**Cholesterol**	20 mg	Sugar	0 g
Calories from Fat 15	**Sodium**	150 mg	**Protein**	11 g
% Daily Value Vitamin A 2%	Vitamin C 2%	Calcium 0%	Iron 0%	

Home-Style Egg Salad

Serves 3
Serving size: ¼ cup (50 mL)

3 large eggs hard-boiled, peeled
¼ tsp (1 mL) celery seed
2 tbsp (30 mL) light mayonnaise
Salt and pepper to taste

Directions:
1. Cut the eggs into quarters.
2. Place eggs and remaining ingredients into mini food chopper and puree for 20 seconds.
3. Using a rubber spatula, scrape down the sides of the bowl and puree an additional 20 seconds or until smooth.

Nutrition Facts	Amount		Amount	
Serves 3	Fat	9 g	Carbohydrate	2 g
Serving size ¼ cup (50 mL)	Saturated Fat	1.5 g	Fiber	0 g
Calories 110	**Cholesterol**	215 mg	Sugar	1 g
Calories from Fat 80	**Sodium**	150 mg	**Protein**	6 g
% Daily Value Vitamin A 6%	Vitamin C 0%	Calcium 2%	Iron 4%	

Quick and Easy Vegetable Chicken Soup

Serves 8
Serving size: ¼ cup (50 mL)

One 18.5-oz (524 mL) can ready-to-serve low sodium vegetable soup
2 oz (55 g) canned chicken, drained
1 tsp (5 mL) low sodium chicken bouillon granules

Directions:
1. Place all ingredients into blender and blend until smooth.
2. Place in a microwave safe bowl and heat covered for 2 minutes; stir.

Note: This soup freezes well for up to 3 months.

Nutrition Facts	Amount		Amount	
Serves 8	**Fat**	0.5 g	**Carbohydrate**	6 g
Serving size ¼ cup (50 mL)	Saturated Fat	0 g	Fiber	1 g
Calories 40	**Cholesterol**	5 mg	Sugar	1 g
Calories from Fat 5	**Sodium**	190 mg	**Protein**	3 g

% Daily Value   Vitamin A 4%   Vitamin C 2%   Calcium 2%   Iron 2%

Sautéed Turkey Cheesy Cups

Serves 6
Serving size: ¼ cup (50 mL)

½ lb (225 g) ground turkey breast, cooked
½ cup (125 mL) fat free cream cheese
½ tsp (2 mL) dried Italian seasoning
1 large egg
½ cup (125 mL) no salt added tomato sauce

Directions:
1. Preheat oven to 350°F (180°C).
2. In mini food chopper combine the ground turkey, fat free cream cheese, seasoning, and egg; puree until turkey mixture is smooth.
3. Spray a 6-cup muffin pan with nonstick cooking spray.
4. Divide mixture into 6 equal portions and place into each muffin cup. Flatten mixture with spoon.
5. Evenly divide tomato sauce over top of turkey mixture.
6. Bake for 12 minutes and tomato sauce is bubbling.

Note: This can be refrigerated and reheated in microwave.

Nutrition Facts	Amount		Amount	
Serves 6	Fat	1.5 g	Carbohydrate	3 g
Serving size ¼ cup (50 mL)	Saturated Fat	0 g	Fiber	0 g
Calories 80	Cholesterol	45 mg	Sugar	2 g
Calories from Fat 15	Sodium	170 mg	Protein	14 g
% Daily Value Vitamin A 4%	Vitamin C 4%	Calcium 8%	Iron 4%	

Slow Cooker Split Pea Soup

Serves 12
Serving size: ¼ cup (50 mL)

3 cups (750 mL) water
1 ½ tsp (7 mL) ham-flavored soup base
4 oz (115 g) dry split peas, rinsed
¼ tsp (2 mL) pepper
1 medium carrot, chopped
1 medium celery stalk, chopped
One 8-oz (250 mL) can no salt added tomatoes, do not drain
¼ tsp (1 mL) ground cumin
1 tsp (5 mL) garlic powder
1 small onion, chopped

Directions:
1. Place all ingredients into slow cooker.
2. Turn on low and let cook for at least 8 hours.
3. Place soup into blender* in small batches and blend until smooth.

*Use a blender for this recipe since it is a liquid.
Note: This soup freezes well for up to 3 months.

Nutrition Facts	Amount		Amount	
Serves 12	**Fat**	0 g	**Carbohydrate**	8 g
Serving size ¼ cup (50 mL)	Saturated Fat	0 g	Fiber	3 g
Calories 45	**Cholesterol**	0 mg	Sugar	2 g
Calories from Fat 0	**Sodium**	200 mg	**Protein**	3 g
% Daily Value Vitamin A 20%	Vitamin C 4%	Calcium 2%	Iron 4%	

Wendy's Chili

Serves 4
Serving size: ¼ cup (50 mL)

1 order small Wendy's chili, no toppings

Directions:
1. Place chili in blender and blend for 30 seconds or until smooth.

Enjoy!

Note: We have included this recipe for those days when you have not had the time or energy to prepare a meal for yourself.

Nutrition Facts	Amount		Amount	
Serves 4	**Fat**	1.5 g	**Carbohydrate**	5 g
Serving size ¼ cup (50 mL)	Saturated Fat	0.5 g	Fiber	1 g
Calories 110	**Cholesterol**	10 mg	Sugar	1 g
Calories from Fat 15	**Sodium**	220 mg	**Protein**	4 g

% Daily Value   Vitamin A 4%   Vitamin C 2%   Calcium 2%   Iron 2%

Smooth Food Dinners

Calypso Seafood Salad

Serves 4
Serving size: ¼ cup (50 mL)

4 oz (115 g) cooked crabmeat
4 oz (115 g) cooked shrimp, peeled and deveined
2 tbsp (30 mL) seafood cocktail sauce
1 tbsp (15 mL) light sour cream
½ tsp (2 mL) onion powder
1 tsp (5 mL) lime juice
1 clove fresh garlic

Directions:
1. Place all ingredients into a mini food chopper.
2. Blend for 20 seconds.
3. Using a rubber spatula, scrape down sides of the bowl; puree for an additional 30 seconds.

Note: Store in an airtight container. It will keep its freshness for two days.

Nutrition Facts	Amount		Amount	
Serves 4	**Fat**	1 g	**Carbohydrate**	3 g
Serving size ¼ cup (50 mL)	Saturated Fat	0 g	Fiber	0 g
Calories 80	**Cholesterol**	100 mg	Sugar	0 g
Calories from Fat 10	**Sodium**	480 mg	**Protein**	12 g
% Daily Value Vitamin A 0%	Vitamin C 4%	Calcium 8%	Iron 4%	

Cheesy Refried Beans

Serves 1
Serving size: ¼ cup (50 mL)

¼ cup (50 mL) canned vegetarian refried beans
2 tbsp (30 mL) shredded reduced fat sharp cheddar cheese
1 tbsp (15 mL) mild taco sauce

Directions:
1. Put refried beans in a small microwavable bowl.
2. Sprinkle the cheese on top of the refried beans; sprinkle taco sauce over top of cheese.
3. Microwave uncovered for 45 seconds or until hot.

Nutrition Facts	Amount		Amount	
Serves 1	**Fat**	1 g	**Carbohydrate**	10 g
Serving size ¼ cup (50 mL)	Saturated Fat	0.5 g	Fiber	3 g
Calories 70	**Cholesterol**	5 mg	Sugar	1 g
Calories from Fat 10	**Sodium**	470 mg	**Protein**	7 g

% Daily Value   Vitamin A 0%   Vitamin C 0%   Calcium 8%   Iron 6%

Dilled Salmon Cucumber Dip

Serves 3
Serving size: ¼ cup (50 mL)

One 5-oz (145 g) vacuum sealed pouch salmon*
1 tbsp (15 mL) peeled and chopped cucumber
½ tsp (2 mL) lemon juice
2 tbsp (30 mL) light mayonnaise
1 tsp (5 mL) chopped fresh dill
Salt and pepper to taste

Directions:
1. Remove salmon from pouch and place in mini food chopper.
2. Add remaining ingredients to mini food chopper.
3. Blend for 20 seconds.
4. Using a rubber spatula, scrape down sides of the bowl; puree for an additional 30 seconds.

* Chef Dave's taste preference is the salmon that comes in the pouch.

Nutrition Facts	Amount		Amount	
Serves 3	**Fat**	4.5 g	**Carbohydrate**	1 g
Serving size ¼ cup (50 mL)	Saturated Fat	0.5 g	Fiber	0 g
Calories 80	**Cholesterol**	30 mg	Sugar	0 g
Calories from Fat 40	**Sodium**	230 mg	**Protein**	12 g
% Daily Value Vitamin A 0%	Vitamin C 0% Calcium 0%		Iron 2%	

Ginger Sesame Ground Chicken

Serves 4
Serving size: ¼ cup (50 mL)

½ lb (225 g) ground chicken breast
½ tsp (2 mL) sesame oil
¼ tsp (1 mL) chopped garlic
¼ tsp (1 mL) ground ginger
¼ tsp (1 mL) salt
¼ tsp (1 mL) pepper

Directions:
1. In a medium sauté pan over medium heat, add all ingredients and sauté for 5 minutes or until temperature reaches 165°F (75°C).
2. Drain excess fat.
3. Place chicken in mini food chopper and blend until smooth.

Nutrition Facts	Amount		Amount	
Serves 4	**Fat**	1 g	**Carbohydrate**	0 g
Serving size ¼ cup (50 mL)	Saturated Fat	0 g	Fiber	0 g
Calories 70	**Cholesterol**	35 mg	Sugar	0 g
Calories from Fat 10	**Sodium**	35 mg	**Protein**	13 g

% Daily Value   Vitamin A 0%   Vitamin C 2%   Calcium 0%   Iron 2%

Greek Scramble

Serves 1
Serving size: ¼ cup (50 mL)

¼ tsp (1 mL) olive oil
1 large egg, whisked
1 tsp (5 mL) reduced fat feta cheese crumbles
½ tsp (2 mL) chopped black olives
¼ tsp (1 mL) garlic powder
½ tsp (2 mL) chopped fresh cilantro

Directions:
1. Heat oil in a small sauté pan over medium heat.
2. When oil is hot, add egg, feta, olives, garlic, and cilantro.
3. Using a plastic spatula, stir egg mixture until soft and fluffy, approximately 2 minutes.

Note: To reduce cholesterol, omit egg and use ¼ cup (50 mL) egg substitute.

Nutrition Facts	Amount		Amount	
Serves 1	Fat	6 g	Carbohydrate	2 g
Serving size ¼ cup (50 mL)	Saturated Fat	1.5 g	Fiber	0 g
Calories 100	**Cholesterol**	180 mg	Sugar	2 g
Calories from Fat 50	**Sodium**	135 mg	**Protein**	7 g

% Daily Value   Vitamin A 6%   Vitamin C 0%   Calcium 4%   Iron 6%

Italian Sausage Bake

Serves 4
Serving size: ¼ cup (50 mL)

½ lb (225 g) fresh ground turkey Italian sausage, remove sausage from casing if using links
¼ cup (50 mL) no salt added tomato sauce
¼ tsp (1 mL) chopped garlic
¼ tsp (1 mL) onion powder
¼ cup (50 mL) shredded part skim mozzarella cheese

Directions:
1. Preheat oven to 350°F (180°C).
2. In a medium sauté pan over high heat, add sausage.
3. Sauté until sausage is browned; drain excess fat.
4. Place sausage into mini food chopper and blend until ground into very small pieces.
5. Add tomato sauce, garlic, and onion powder and blend until smooth.
6. Place in a small baking dish, cover with cheese, and bake in oven until cheese has melted, about 10 minutes.

Nutrition Facts	Amount		Amount	
Serves 4	**Fat**	7 g	**Carbohydrate**	2 g
Serving size ¼ cup (50 mL)	Saturated Fat	1 g	Fiber	0 g
Calories 120	**Cholesterol**	35 mg	Sugar	2 g
Calories from Fat 70	**Sodium**	420 mg	**Protein**	11 g
% Daily Value Vitamin A 2%	Vitamin C 4%	Calcium 6%	Iron 6%	

Simple Turkey Chili

Serves 8
Serving size: ¼ cup (50 mL)

½ lb (225 g) ground turkey breast
1 tsp (1 mL) chopped garlic
¼ cup (50 mL) chopped onions
1 cup (250 mL) no salt added tomato sauce
1 cup (250 mL) drained no salt added diced tomatoes
1 tsp (5 mL) chili powder
½ tsp (2 mL) ground cumin
¼ tsp (1 mL) pepper
½ cup (125 mL) drained canned black beans

Directions:
1. Place ground turkey into a medium pot and sauté for 5 minutes; drain fat.
2. Add remaining ingredients and bring to a simmer. Let simmer for 20 minutes.
3. Place chili into food processor and blend until smooth.

Note: This chili can be frozen for up to 3 months.

Nutrition Facts	Amount		Amount	
Serves 8	**Fat**	0.5 g	**Carbohydrate**	7 g
Serving size ¼ cup (50 mL)	Saturated Fat	0 g	Fiber	2 g
Calories 70	**Cholesterol**	10 mg	Sugar	3 g
Calories from Fat 5	**Sodium**	85 mg	**Protein**	9 g

% Daily Value   Vitamin A 8%   Vitamin C 10%   Calcium 2%   Iron 6%

Slow Cooker Lentil Soup

Serves 12
Serving size: ¼ cup (50 mL)

3 cups (750 mL) water
1 ½ tsp (7 mL) ham-flavored soup base
4 oz (115 g) dry lentils, rinsed
¼ tsp (1 mL) pepper
1 medium carrot, chopped
1 medium celery stalk, chopped
One 8-oz (250 mL) can no salt added tomatoes, do not drain
1 tsp (5 mL) garlic powder
1 small onion, chopped
Salt and pepper to taste

Directions:
1. Place all ingredients into a slow cooker.
2. Turn on low and let cook for at least 8 hours.
3. Place soup into blender* in small batches and blend until smooth.

*Use a blender for this recipe since it is a liquid.

Note: This soup freezes well for up to 3 months.

Nutrition Facts	Amount		Amount	
Serves 12	**Fat**	0.5 g	**Carbohydrate**	8 g
Serving size ¼ cup (50 mL)	Saturated Fat	0 g	Fiber	2 g
Calories 45	**Cholesterol**	0 mg	Sugar	1 g
Calories from Fat 5	**Sodium**	200 mg	**Protein**	2 g
% Daily Value Vitamin A 20%	Vitamin C 4%	Calcium 2%	Iron 4%	

Spicy Tuna Spread

Serves 3
Serving size: ¼ cup (50 mL)

One 6-oz (170 g) can water-packed tuna, drained
2 tbsp (30 mL) chopped fresh dill weed
1 tsp (5 mL) hot sauce
1 tsp (5 mL) minced garlic
1 tbsp (15 mL) fresh lemon juice
2 tbsp (30 mL) light sour cream
2 tbsp (30 mL) light mayonnaise

Directions:
1. Place tuna, dill, hot sauce, garlic, and lemon juice in a mini food chopper.
2. Puree for 20 seconds.
3. Using a rubber spatula, scrape down the sides of the bowl.
4. Add the sour cream and mayonnaise, and puree for another 30 seconds.

Nutrition Facts	Amount		Amount	
Serves 3	**Fat**	5 g	**Carbohydrate**	2 g
Serving size ¼ cup (50 mL)	Saturated Fat	1 g	Fiber	0 g
Calories 110	**Cholesterol**	35 mg	Sugar	1 g
Calories from Fat 45	**Sodium**	380 mg	**Protein**	14 g
% Daily Value Vitamin A 2%	Vitamin C 6%	Calcium 2%	Iron 0%	

Taco Stuffing

Serves 4
Serving size: ¼ cup (50 mL)

½ lb (225 g) lean ground beef
½ tsp (2 mL) garlic powder
½ tsp (2 mL) onion powder
½ tsp (2 mL) chili powder
¼ tsp (1 mL) ground cumin
¼ tsp (1 mL) salt
¼ cup (50 mL) water
2 tbsp (30 mL) shredded reduced fat sharp cheddar cheese
2 tsp (10 mL) fat free sour cream

Directions:
1. In a medium sauté pan over medium heat, add ground beef.
2. Brown ground beef; drain off any excess fat.
3. Add dry seasonings and water; bring to a simmer and cook for 2 minutes.
4. Remove from heat and place into mini food chopper, add cheese.
5. Puree for 20 seconds.
6. Top with sour cream.

Nutrition Facts	Amount		Amount	
Serves 4	**Fat**	6 g	**Carbohydrate**	1 g
Serving size ¼ cup (50 mL)	Saturated Fat	2.5 g	Fiber	0 g
Calories 110	**Cholesterol**	40 mg	Sugar	0 g
Calories from Fat 50	**Sodium**	210 mg	**Protein**	13 g

% Daily Value   Vitamin A 2%   Vitamin C 0%   Calcium 4%   Iron 8%

SOFT FOODS

A Note from Vicki

By now, you are probably anxious to eat foods with more texture. It's time to start the next step of your diet progression. Your pouch is healing, and you still need to practice caution with the foods you select. The soft food step usually starts 2 to 4 weeks after weight loss surgery. Follow this step of the diet for 1 to 4 weeks before starting "regular" foods. Rushing to eat regular foods too soon can cause nausea, food sticking, discomfort, and possible vomiting. Always follow the recommendations given to you by your bariatric health care provider.

Soft foods are exactly that. They should be easy to chew. A soft food should be easily mashed with a fork. You may not be accustomed to eating your vegetables cooked this soft and eventually you will be able to eat some raw vegetables. Think of feeding your pouch as if you would feed a baby. You wouldn't give a baby a tossed salad and steak!

Many of the recipes from Part 2: Smooth Foods will work great for this step of the diet. Just don't puree them in the mini food chopper.

You may still have difficulty meeting your protein goal. Most of these recipes follow the guideline of protein first. Since your portions are still limited, you may need to eat more frequently, 4 to 6 times a day. Remember to take small bites. Soft foods have more texture, so it is especially important to remember to chew each bite 20 to 30 times. No one enjoys having food stuck. Remember not to drink beverages with your meals, and wait 30 to 60 minutes after you finish eating before drinking.

The recipes in this book have portions adjusted for this step of the diet, but your portion size may vary depending on your type of weight loss surgery. As time goes on and you prepare these recipes again, you may find that you are able to eat more than what we have specified. It is important that you do not overfill your pouch as this can cause discomfort.

Enjoy the weight loss success you have already achieved. You are probably feeling better and have more energy. Following the guidelines will bring you long-term success. These recipes can be used for a lifetime . . . your new lifetime of a healthier, happier you.

Eat Smart . . .
Vicki Bovee, MS, RD, LD

A Note from Chef Dave

Soft foods are the step after smooth foods. Soft foods are foods that require a little more chewing. These foods help you get accustomed to chewing your food enough to swallow without it getting stuck or causing discomfort. In addition, soft foods offer more choices and help get you on the right track to eating larger cut of meats and vegetables when your surgeon says you are ready.

It's important to plan for your soft food step. Ground meats such as pork, beef, chicken, and lamb are all great choices. Flaky fish and seafood, such as crab and diced shrimp, are great too. Fruits and vegetables should be purchased and eaten within the same week. When you eat fruits and vegetables, remove the peel to help ease chewing and digestion. Also, cut your fruits and vegetables up into bite-size pieces no bigger than the tip of your little finger.

The deli is a place that helps with soft food preparation. Choose deli meats that are the least processed and low in sodium. Requesting the meats be shaved rather than sliced will make them easier to eat. Most delis also have rotisserie chicken, which is perfect for pulling the meat from the bone and then shredding into small bite-size pieces.

Don't forget the cheese, which is an easy way to get protein. Cheese is a little higher in fat, unless you go for the reduced fat cheeses.

I also find that having the "right tools for the right job" not only shortens prep time, but also makes the actual meal preparation a breeze. Here is a list of must haves in your kitchen for the soft food stage:

- large cutting board
- 6-inch chef knife for chopping
- food processor with interchangeable cutting disk for slicing, grating, and chopping foods
- cheese grater for small prep jobs such as grating carrots, eggs, and cheese.

As your chef, I wouldn't be doing my job if I did not mention food safety. I find that because most weight loss surgery patients eat less, they tend to keep the leftover foods for days and even as long as a week, not wanting to waste food. This is dangerous because it can cause food poisoning and make you very sick. It is recommended when storing food, to keep it in an airtight container in the refrigerator and do not keep longer than three days. When in doubt throw it out!

Cook Smart . . .
Chef Dave Fouts

Soft Food Breakfasts

Basil, Tomato, Cream Cheese Frittata

Serves 6
Serving size: 1 piece (170 g)

3 cups (750 mL) egg substitute
¼ tsp (1 mL) dried sage
¼ tsp (1 mL) dried oregano
¼ tsp (1 mL) dried thyme
1 tsp (5 mL) butter
3 medium plum tomatoes, sliced
1 cup (250 mL) fresh basil leaves, finely chopped
6 oz (170 g) fat free cream cheese, cubed

Directions:
1. Whisk together egg substitute, sage, oregano, and thyme.
2. In large skillet, melt butter over medium heat. Add tomatoes and sauté one minute.
3. Lower heat and add basil sautéing until limp, 1 to 2 minutes.
4. Pour egg mixture over all and top with cream cheese cubes.
5. Cover and cook over low heat approximately 20 minutes or until set on top.
6. Cut into 6 equal pieces to serve.

Nutrition Facts	Amount		Amount	
Serves 6	Fat	5 g	Carbohydrate	4 g
Serving size 1 piece (170 g)	Saturated Fat	1.5 g	Fiber	1 g
Calories 150	**Cholesterol**	5 mg	Sugar	3 g
Calories from Fat 45	**Sodium**	430 mg	**Protein**	20 g
% Daily Value Vitamin A 25%	Vitamin C 8%	Calcium 20%	Iron 15%	

Berrycotta Pancakes

Serves 6
Serving size: 2 pancakes (170 g)

¾ cup (175 mL) whole wheat flour
¾ cup (175 mL) all-purpose flour
1 tsp (5 mL) baking powder
¼ tsp (1 mL) baking soda
¼ tsp (1 mL) salt
1 ½ tsp (7 mL) sugar
2 tbsp (30 mL) butter, melted

¾ cup (175 mL) part skim ricotta cheese
1 large egg
½ cup (125 mL) orange juice
1 cup (250 mL) fat free milk
½ tsp (2 mL) vanilla extract
1 cup (250 mL) blueberries, fresh or frozen

Directions:
1. In a bowl, combine the flours with baking powder, soda, salt, and sugar.
2. In another bowl, whisk together the butter, ricotta cheese, egg, orange juice, milk, and vanilla.
3. Combine the wet and dry ingredients just until blended.
4. Gently stir in the blueberries.
5. Spray a skillet or griddle with nonstick cooking spray. Heat over medium heat.
6. Spoon ¼ cup (50 mL) of batter for each pancake onto the hot skillet.
7. Cook about 2 minutes or until browned on the underside, then flip the pancake.
8. Cook until golden brown.

Nutrition Facts	Amount		Amount	
Serves 6	Fat	7 g	Carbohydrate	33 g
Serving size 2 pancakes (170 g)	Saturated Fat	4 g	Fiber	3 g
Calories 230	**Cholesterol**	50 mg	Sugar	6 g
Calories from Fat 70	**Sodium**	330 mg	**Protein**	10 g
% Daily Value	Vitamin A 8%	Vitamin C 20%	Calcium 20%	Iron 8%

Fluffy French Toast with Strawberries

Serves 4
Serving size: 1 slice each (170 g)

1 cup (250 mL) egg substitute
⅔ cup (150 mL) fat free milk
½ tsp (2 mL) vanilla extract
½ tsp (2 mL) cinnamon
4 slices whole wheat bread
1 cup (250 mL) frozen, unsweetened strawberries, thawed

Directions:
1. Whisk together egg substitute, milk, vanilla, and cinnamon until light and frothy.
2. Dip bread slices in egg mixture and place on a baking pan sprayed with a nonstick cooking spray.
3. Pour any leftover mixture over bread slices; cover and refrigerate overnight.
4. Next day, sauté bread on nonstick griddle until light brown and crispy.
5. Top with strawberries.

Note: Sugar free syrup can be used if desired.

Nutrition Facts	Amount		Amount	
Serves 4	**Fat**	4 g	**Carbohydrate**	20 g
Serving size 1 slice (170 g)	Saturated Fat	0.5 g	Fiber	3 g
Calories 170	**Cholesterol**	0 mg	Sugar	7 g
Calories from Fat 35	**Sodium**	260 mg	**Protein**	13 g
% Daily Value Vitamin A 6%	Vitamin C 40%	Calcium 15%	Iron 15%	

Peanut Butter Shredded Wheat Cereal

Serves 1
Serving size: ¾ cup (175 mL)

1 large shredded wheat biscuit, broken into chunks
½ cup (125 mL) 1 % milk, heated
1 tsp (5 mL) creamy peanut butter
2 packets sugar substitute sweetener
¼ tsp (2 mL) vanilla extract

Directions:
1. Place all ingredients into a small bowl.
2. Cover; heat in microwave for 2 minutes.
3. Let sit for 1 minute.
4. Serve warm.

Nutrition Facts	Amount		Amount	
Serves 1	**Fat**	5 g	Carbohydrate	29 g
Serving size ¾ cup (175 mL)	Saturated Fat	1.5 g	Fiber	3 g
Calories 190	**Cholesterol**	10 mg	Sugar	9 g
Calories from Fat 45	**Sodium**	110 mg	**Protein**	10 g
% Daily Value Vitamin A 6%	Vitamin C 2%	Calcium 20%	Iron 4%	

Pear-Spiced Oatmeal Bread Pudding

Serves 8
Serving size: 1 piece (190 g)

6 slices day-old whole wheat bread, cubed
¾ cup (175 mL) quick cooking oats, uncooked
1 cup (250 mL) egg substitute, beaten
2 cups (500 mL) canned pears, in juice, drained and diced
2 ½ cups (625 mL) fat free milk
¼ cup (50 mL) sugar substitute (Splenda)
1 tbsp (30 mL) vanilla extract
1 tbsp (30 mL) apple pie spice

Directions:

1. Preheat oven to 350°F (180°C).
2. Place cubed day-old bread in a large bowl.
3. Add oatmeal, egg substitute, pears, milk, sugar substitute, vanilla, and apple pie spice to bread cubes and mix well.
4. Place mixture in a small 8-inch x 8-inch baking dish that has been sprayed with nonstick cooking spray.
5. Bake until pudding has risen high and is medium brown, about 30 minutes. It will rise like a soufflé and fall as it cools.
6. Cut into 8 equal pieces to serve.

Nutrition Facts	Amount		Amount	
Serves 8	**Fat**	2.5 g	**Carbohydrate**	29 g
Serving size 1 piece (190 g)	Saturated Fat	0 g	Fiber	4 g
Calories 180	**Cholesterol**	0 mg	Sugar	11 g
Calories from Fat 20	**Sodium**	210 mg	**Protein**	10 g
% Daily Value Vitamin A 6%	Vitamin C 0%	Calcium 10%	Iron 10%	

Sausage and Potato Skillet

Serves 6
Serving size: ¾ cup (175 mL)

2 tsp (10 mL) canola oil
2 small onions, sliced thin
1 lb (455 g) turkey Italian sausage, remove casings if using links
½ lb (225 g) potatoes, peeled and sliced thin
1 tbsp (15 mL) yellow prepared mustard
1 cup (250 mL) low sodium chicken broth
Pepper to taste

Directions:
1. In large frying pan with a lid, heat canola oil.
2. Add onions and sausage. Sauté for 5 minutes.
3. Add potatoes; stir into onion and sausage mixture.
4. Continue cooking until potatoes begin to brown.
5. Add mustard and chicken broth; cover with lid, and cook for 10 minutes or until potatoes are tender.
6. Remove lid and add pepper to taste.

Nutrition Facts	Amount		Amount	
Serves 6	**Fat**	10 g	**Carbohydrate**	9 g
Serving size ¾ cup (175 mL)	Saturated Fat	0 g	Fiber	1 g
Calories 180	**Cholesterol**	45 mg	Sugar	2 g
Calories from Fat 90	**Sodium**	530 mg	**Protein**	15 g

% Daily Value   Vitamin A 0%   Vitamin C 20%   Calcium 2%   Iron 10%

Summer Squash and Sausage Frittata

Serves 6
Serving size: 1 piece (140 g)

8 oz (225 g) veggie sausage links, thawed and chopped
3 cups (750 mL) shredded, unpeeled yellow squash
2 green onions, chopped
1 tbsp (15 mL) minced fresh basil
1 tsp (5 mL) Italian seasoning
1 cup (250 mL) egg substitute
⅓ cup (75 mL) fat free milk
2 oz (55 g) light cream cheese, diced into ½-inch cubes
¼ cup (50 mL) shredded reduced fat sharp cheddar cheese

Directions:
1. Preheat oven to 325°F (160°C).
2. In a medium skillet sprayed with a nonstick coating, brown veggie sausage. Spread over bottom of an 8-inch x 8-inch pan sprayed with nonstick cooking spray.
3. Layer squash over sausage; sprinkle green onions and seasonings over top.
4. Whisk egg substitute with milk and pour over squash and sausage.
5. Sprinkle with cream cheese cubes and top with cheddar cheese.
6. Bake for 45 minutes until top is lightly golden or knife inserted in center comes out clean.
7. Cut into 6 equal pieces to serve.

Nutrition Facts	Amount		Amount	
Serves 6	**Fat**	6 g	**Carbohydrate**	9 g
Serving size 1 piece (140 g)	Saturated Fat	2 g	Fiber	3 g
Calories 160	**Cholesterol**	10 mg	Sugar	2 g
Calories from Fat 60	**Sodium**	390 mg	**Protein**	16 g
% Daily Value Vitamin A 8%	Vitamin C 10%	Calcium 10%	Iron 15%	

Swiss Oatmeal

Serves 4
Serving size: ½ cup (125 mL)

½ cup (125 mL) old-fashioned rolled oats
½ cup (125 mL) fat free, 1 %, or calcium fortified soy milk
½ tsp (2 mL) cinnamon
1 medium banana, sliced
¾ cup (175 mL) Greek nonfat plain yogurt
1 tsp (5 ml) vanilla extract
Sugar substitute to taste

Directions:

1. Mix oats, milk, and cinnamon in a tightly covered container. Store in the refrigerator overnight or for at least 8 hours.
2. Before serving, stir in remaining ingredients.
3. Serve cold.

Nutrition Facts	Amount		Amount	
Serves 4	**Fat**	1 g	**Carbohydrate**	17 g
Serving size ½ cup (125 mL)	Saturated Fat	0 g	Fiber	2 g
Calories 100	**Cholesterol**	0 mg	Sugar	7 g
Calories from Fat 5	**Sodium**	30 mg	**Protein**	7 g

% Daily Value   Vitamin A 2%   Vitamin C 4%   Calcium 8%   Iron 4%

Three Cheese Mexican Frittata

Serves 4
Serving size: 1 piece (115 g)

6 large eggs, whisked
¼ cup (50 mL) fat free half and half
¼ cup (50 mL) shredded reduced fat Monterey Jack cheese
¼ cup (50 mL) shredded reduced fat swiss cheese
¼ cup (50 mL) shredded reduced fat sharp cheddar cheese
1 tsp (5 mL) seeded and diced jalapeno peppers
¼ cup (50 mL) finely chopped green onions
¼ tsp (1 mL) ground cumin

Directions:
1. Combine all ingredients in a large bowl; set aside.
2. Spray a 10-inch, nonstick skillet with nonstick cooking spray and heat pan over medium heat.
3. Pour ¼ of the egg mixture into the pan and cover. Cook for 3 to 4 minutes until set and lightly browned.
4. Slide out onto a plate, invert the skillet over the frittata on the plate, and flip the frittata back into the skillet.
5. Cover and cook an additional 2 to 3 minutes. Remove to a serving dish and keep warm.
6. Repeat three more times with the remaining mixture.

Nutrition Facts	Amount		Amount	
Serves 6	Fat	9 g	Carbohydrate	5 g
Serving size 1 piece (115 g)	Saturated Fat	3.5 g	Fiber	0 g
Calories 170	**Cholesterol**	280 mg	Sugar	3 g
Calories from Fat 80	**Sodium**	250 mg	**Protein**	15 g
% Daily Value Vitamin A 10%	Vitamin C 2%	Calcium 20%	Iron 8%	

Turkey and Cheddar Omelet

Serves 2
Serving size: ½ omelet (70 g)

2 large eggs
1 tbsp (15 mL) water
2 tsp (10 mL) chopped bell pepper
2 tsp (10 mL) chopped onion
2 tsp (10 mL) chopped tomato
1 oz (30 g) cooked ground turkey breast
2 tsp (10 mL) shredded reduced fat sharp cheddar cheese

Directions:

1. Beat together eggs and water.
2. Spray a 10-inch omelet pan with cooking spray, and place over medium heat.
3. Add bell pepper, onion, and tomato and sauté vegetables for 2 minutes.
4. Pour in egg mixture.
5. With a spatula, carefully push cooked portions at edges toward center so uncooked portions can reach hot pan surfaces, while drawing cooked portions toward center.
6. While top is still moist and creamy looking, place cooked ground turkey and cheese on one side of omelet.
7. With spatula, fold unfilled side of omelet over filling. Cook an additional 1 minute to melt cheese and move to plate.
8. Cut into 2 equal pieces to serve.

Note: I like to use a Teflon-coated pan to keep the omelet from sticking.

Nutrition Facts	Amount		Amount	
Serves 2	**Fat**	4.5 g	**Carbohydrate**	2 g
Serving size 1 piece (70 g)	Saturated Fat	1.5 g	Fiber	0 g
Calories 90	**Cholesterol**	185 mg	Sugar	2 g
Calories from Fat 40	**Sodium**	90 mg	**Protein**	10 g

% Daily Value Vitamin A 6% Vitamin C 6% Calcium 4% Iron 6%

Soft Food Lunches

Beef and Cheddar Sauté

Serves 8
Serving size: ½ cup (125 mL)

1 tsp (5 mL) olive oil
½ lb (115 g) fresh button mushrooms, sliced
1 tbsp (15 mL) chopped garlic
1 lb (455 g) lean ground beef, cooked, drained, and set aside
½ cup (125 mL) beef broth
10 oz (300 g) fresh spinach, stems removed
Pepper to taste
¼ cup (50 mL) shredded reduced fat sharp cheddar cheese

Directions:
1. In a large sauté pan heat oil over medium heat.
2. When oil is hot, add mushrooms and garlic. Sauté until mushrooms are soft, approximately 5 minutes.
3. Add cooked ground beef, beef broth, spinach, and pepper; bring to a simmer.
4. Add cheese. Toss and serve.

Nutrition Facts	Amount		Amount	
Serves 8	**Fat**	7 g	**Carbohydrate**	5 g
Serving size ½ cup (125 mL)	Saturated Fat	2.5 g	Fiber	2 g
Calories 130	**Cholesterol**	40 mg	Sugar	0 g
Calories from Fat 60	**Sodium**	170 mg	**Protein**	14 g
% Daily Value Vitamin A 25%	Vitamin C 10%	Calcium 4%	Iron 15%	

Cajun Chicken Salad

Serves 8
Serving size: ½ cup (125 mL)

1 lb (455 g) boneless, skinless chicken breast
½ tsp (2 mL) red pepper flakes
½ tsp (2 mL) pepper
1 tsp (5 mL) garlic powder
1 tsp (5 mL) chili powder
¼ tsp (1 mL) salt
1 tsp (5 mL) olive oil
¾ cup (175 mL) light mayonnaise
3 tbsp (45 mL) chopped fresh parsley
2 tbsp (30 mL) chopped fresh chives
2 tbsp (30 mL) lemon juice
1 tbsp (15 mL) Dijon mustard

Directions:

1. Rub chicken with red pepper flakes, pepper, garlic powder, chili powder, and salt.
2. In a large skillet, heat oil over medium high heat. When oil is hot, turn heat down to medium, and add chicken.
3. Cook chicken 5 minutes on each side or until internal temperature reaches 165°F (75°C).
4. Let chicken cool. Cut into ¼-inch pieces.
5. In a large mixing bowl, add chicken, mayonnaise, parsley, chives, lemon juice, and mustard; mix well. Cover and refrigerate.

Nutrition Facts	Amount		Amount	
Serves 8	**Fat**	9 g	**Carbohydrate**	4 g
Serving size ½ cup (125 mL)	Saturated Fat	0 g	Fiber	0 g
Calories 150	**Cholesterol**	40 mg	Sugar	0 g
Calories from Fat 80	**Sodium**	330 mg	**Protein**	13 g

% Daily Value   Vitamin A 6%   Vitamin C 8%   Calcium 2%   Iron 4%

Crab Three Bean Salad

Serves 6
Serving size: ½ cup (125 mL)

½ cup (125 mL) canned navy beans, drained and rinsed
½ cup (125 mL) canned garbanzo beans, drained and rinsed
½ cup (125 mL) canned kidney beans, drained and rinsed
1 tbsp (15 mL) olive oil
2 tbsp (30 mL) fresh lemon juice
3 cloves fresh garlic, chopped
1 tbsp (15 mL) chopped fresh dill
4 green onions, finely chopped
½ lb (225 g) cooked crab meat

Directions:
1. Place all ingredients into a medium-size mixing bowl and mix well.
2. Chill and serve.

Note: Cooked shrimp or chicken can be substituted for the crab.

Nutrition Facts	Amount		Amount	
Serves 6	**Fat**	3 g	**Carbohydrate**	12 g
Serving size ½ cup (125 mL)	Saturated Fat	0 g	Fiber	3 g
Calories 120	**Cholesterol**	35 mg	Sugar	1 g
Calories from Fat 30	**Sodium**	300 mg	**Protein**	12 g
% Daily Value Vitamin A 2%	Vitamin C 10%	Calcium 6%	Iron 8%	

Easy Cheesy Bean Bake

Serves 6
Serving size: ¾ cup (175 mL)

1 tsp (5 mL) olive oil
2 cloves fresh garlic, minced
½ cup (125 mL) diced onion
¼ cup (50 mL) diced green pepper
1 cup (250 mL) diced tomato
1 tsp (5 mL) dried thyme
One 14.5-oz (425 g) can no salt added navy beans, rinsed and drained
One 14.5-oz (425 g) can no salt added pinto beans, rinsed and drained
½ cup (125 mL) low-sodium vegetable broth
1 cup (250 mL) shredded reduced fat sharp cheddar cheese

Directions:
1. Preheat oven to 325°F (160° C). Coat an 8-inch x 8-inch ovenproof pan with nonstick cooking spray.
2. Heat oil in a medium sauté pan over medium-high heat. Add the garlic, onion, green pepper, tomato, and thyme and sauté for 3 minutes.
3. Add the beans and broth and bring to a simmer for 3 minutes.
4. Pour the bean mixture into the pan. Top with cheese and bake for 30 minutes, or until cheese is bubbly. Let stand to thicken slightly and serve.

Nutrition Facts	Amount		Amount	
Serves 6	**Fat**	2.5 g	**Carbohydrate**	24 g
Serving size ¾ cup (175 mL)	Saturated Fat	1 g	Fiber	8 g
Calories 170	**Cholesterol**	5 mg	Sugar	2 g
Calories from Fat 20	**Sodium**	150 mg	**Protein**	12 g
% Daily Value Vitamin A 6%	Vitamin C 15%	Calcium 15%	Iron 15%	

Flaky Sautéed Cod

Serves 4
Serving size: 6 oz (170 g)

1 lb (455 g) cod, cut into 4 pieces
½ tsp (2 mL) salt
½ tsp (2 mL) pepper
2 tsp (10 mL) dried thyme
1 tsp (5 mL) paprika
2 tsp (10 mL) Wondra Quick-Mixing Flour
2 tsp (10 mL) olive oil
¼ cup (50 mL) no sugar added apple juice
¼ cup (50 mL) sliced fresh mushrooms
¼ cup (50 mL) chopped green onions
1 clove fresh garlic, chopped
½ cup (125 mL) low sodium chicken broth

Directions:
1. Salt and pepper cod. Add thyme and paprika to flour; lightly coat cod with seasoned flour.
2. In large sauté pan, heat oil over medium high heat. When oil is hot, add coated fish and sauté until golden brown.
3. When browned on both sides, add apple juice to deglaze the pan.
4. Add mushrooms and onions, garlic and chicken broth to pan.
5. Simmer for 10 minutes or until fish is cooked. The broth will thicken while cooking.

Nutrition Facts	Amount		Amount	
Serves 4	**Fat**	3.5 g	**Carbohydrate**	5 g
Serving size 6 oz (170 g)	Saturated Fat	0.5 g	Fiber	1 g
Calories 140	**Cholesterol**	40 mg	Sugar	2 g
Calories from Fat 30	**Sodium**	380 mg	**Protein**	21 g
% Daily Value Vitamin A 8%	Vitamin C 10%	Calcium 2%	Iron 8%	

Greek Meatballs

Serves 8
Serving size: 3 meatballs with sauce (170 g)

½ lb (225 g) ground lamb
½ lb (225 g) ground turkey breast
¼ cup (50 mL) seasoned bread crumbs
½ cup (125 mL) reduced fat feta cheese
2 tbsp (30 mL) chopped fresh parsley
¼ cup (125 mL) low sodium beef broth
2 cloves garlic, minced
¼ tsp (1 mL) salt
¼ tsp (1 mL) pepper
3 cups (750 mL) no salt added tomato sauce

Directions:
1. In a large bowl, thoroughly combine ground lamb, turkey, bread crumbs, feta cheese, parsley, beef broth, garlic, salt, and pepper and mix well.
2. Make 24, 1-inch meatballs with your hands.
3. In a large pot, add tomato sauce and bring to a light simmer.
4. Add meatballs to sauce, cover, and let simmer for 25 minutes or until meatballs are thoroughly cooked. **Do not stir** for 10 minutes or meatballs will break apart.

Note: Ground turkey breast can be substituted for ground lamb.

Nutrition Facts	Amount		Amount	
Serves 8	**Fat**	8 g	**Carbohydrate**	11 g
Serving size 3 meatballs (170 g)	Saturated Fat	3.5 g	Fiber	2 g
Calories 170	**Cholesterol**	35 mg	Sugar	5 g
Calories from Fat 70	**Sodium**	200 mg	**Protein**	14 g
% Daily Value Vitamin A 10%	Vitamin C 20%	Calcium 4%	Iron 10%	

Shrimp Manhattan Soup

Serves 6
Serving size: ¾ cup (175 mL)

1 tbsp (15 mL) canola oil
1 small onion, thinly sliced
1 clove garlic, minced
¼ cup (50 mL) chopped green onion
¼ cup (50 mL) diced green bell pepper
1¼ cups (300 mL) no salt added tomato sauce
1 cup (250 mL) low sodium chicken broth
¼ tsp (1 mL) dried thyme
¼ tsp (1 mL) dried rosemary
¼ tsp (1 mL) pepper
1 bay leaf
¼ cup (50 mL) chopped fresh parsley
1 lb (455 g) small shrimp, peeled and deveined

Directions:
1. In a medium pot heat oil over medium high heat, add onions, garlic, and green onions. Cook, covered, over low heat until soft.
2. Add bell pepper, tomato sauce, chicken broth, thyme, rosemary, pepper, and bay leaf; cover and simmer for 1 hour.
3. Add parsley and shrimp. Bring to a simmer; cover for 8 to 10 minutes or until seafood is cooked. Discard bay leaf before serving.

Nutrition Facts	Amount		Amount	
Serves 6	Fat	4 g	Carbohydrate	8 g
Serving size ¾ cup (175 mL)	Saturated Fat	0.5 g	Fiber	1 g
Calories 140	Cholesterol	115 mg	Sugar	4 g
Calories from Fat 35	Sodium	130 mg	Protein	17 g
% Daily Value Vitamin A 15%	Vitamin C 30%	Calcium 6%	Iron 15%	

Swedish Meatballs

Serves 8
Serving size: 3 meatballs with sauce (115 g)

¼ lb (115 g) ground pork
¾ lb (340 g) ground turkey breast
1 large egg
¼ cup (50 mL) grated Parmesan cheese
1 tsp (5 mL) dried basil
1 tsp (5 mL) dried oregano
1 tsp (5 mL) dried thyme
1 tsp (5 mL) garlic powder
1 tsp (5 mL) onion powder

Sauce:
1 cup (250 mL) fat free sour cream
½ cup (125 mL) fat free half and half
2 tbsp (30 mL) sodium free beef bouillon granules
1 tsp (5 mL) garlic powder

Directions:
1. Preheat oven to 350°F (180°C).
2. In a large mixing bowl, combine ground pork, turkey, egg, Parmesan cheese, and spices; mix well.
3. With your hands, roll meatball mixture into 24—1 inch round meatballs; place on baking sheet.
4. Bake for 20 minutes. Remove from oven and set aside.
5. In a medium pot over medium heat, combine sour cream, half and half, beef bouillon and garlic powder.
6. Stir constantly until mixture begins to simmer lightly. Add meatballs and let simmer on low for 5 minutes.

Note: It is very important to stir the sour cream sauce constantly and not let it come to a boil, because the sauce will burn and separate.

Nutrition Facts	Amount		Amount	
Serves 8	**Fat**	5 g	**Carbohydrate**	9 g
Serving size 3 meatballs (115 g)	Saturated Fat	2 g	Fiber	0 g
Calories 160	**Cholesterol**	55 mg	Sugar	4 g
Calories from Fat 45	**Sodium**	140 mg	**Protein**	18 g

% Daily Value   Vitamin A 6%   Vitamin C 2%   Calcium 15%   Iron 6%

Vegetable Beef Soup

Serves 6
Serving size: ¾ cup (175 mL)

1 lb (455 g) lean ground beef
1 cup (250 mL) chopped onion
1 cup (250 mL) sliced carrots
¼ cup (50 mL) chopped red bell pepper
1 cup (250 mL) sliced fresh mushrooms
1 medium tomato, chopped
¼ cup (50 mL) red wine
2 cups (500 mL) low sodium beef broth
1 bay leaf
Pinch hot red pepper flakes
¼ cup (50 mL) chopped fresh parsley
¼ tsp (1 mL) pepper

Directions:
1. In a large heavy pot, combine beef, onion, carrots, red pepper, mushrooms, tomatoes, wine, broth, bay leaf, and red pepper flakes.
2. Cover and simmer over low heat for 1 to 1 ½ hours, stirring occasionally.
3. Stir in parsley and black pepper.
4. Cover and cook 10 minutes, stirring occasionally. Discard bay leaf before serving.

Nutrition Facts	Amount		Amount	
Serves 6	**Fat**	8 g	**Carbohydrate**	7 g
Serving size ¾ cup (175 mL)	Saturated Fat	3 g	Fiber	2 g
Calories 180	**Cholesterol**	50 mg	Sugar	4 g
Calories from Fat 70	**Sodium**	90 mg	**Protein**	18 g
% Daily Value Vitamin A 80%	Vitamin C 30%	Calcium 4%	Iron 15%	

Zesty Lemon Garlic Egg Salad

Serves 6
Serving size: ⅓ cup (75 mL)

6 large hard-boiled eggs, peeled and chopped fine
½ tsp (2 mL) celery seed
1 clove fresh garlic, minced
1 tsp (5 mL) chopped fresh dill
1 tsp (5 mL) fresh lemon juice
¼ cup (50 mL) light mayonnaise
¼ cup (50 mL) nonfat plain yogurt
Salt and pepper to taste

Directions:
1. Place all ingredients into a medium mixing bowl.
2. Mix well.
3. Chill before serving.

Nutrition Facts	Amount		Amount	
Serves 6	**Fat**	9 g	**Carbohydrate**	3 g
Serving size ⅓ cup (75 mL)	Saturated Fat	1.5 g	Fiber	0 g
Calories 120	**Cholesterol**	215 mg	Sugar	1 g
Calories from Fat 80	**Sodium**	150 mg	**Protein**	7 g

% Daily Value   Vitamin A 6%   Vitamin C 2%   Calcium 4%   Iron 4%

Soft Food Dinners

Home-Style Hamburger Skillet

Serves 6
Serving size: ¾ cup (175 mL)

½ lb (225 g) lean ground beef
One 16-oz (455 g) can no salt added cut green beans, drained
One 16-oz (455 g) can no salt added can potatoes, drained, sliced thin
One 14.5-oz (425 g) can no salt added diced tomatoes
¼ cup (50 mL) chopped green onion
½ tsp (2 mL) garlic powder
½ tsp (2 mL) onion powder
Pepper to taste

Directions:
1. Heat a large nonstick skillet over medium high heat.
2. Add ground beef and cook until gray. *Do NOT cook until brown. Brown ground beef crumbles are overcooked, and ground beef crumbles will be difficult to digest.*
3. Add vegetables and seasonings to skillet and heat through.

Nutrition Facts	Amount		Amount	
Serves 6	**Fat**	4 g	**Carbohydrate**	17 g
Serving size ¾ cup (175 mL)	Saturated Fat	1.5 g	Fiber	4 g
Calories 140	**Cholesterol**	25 mg	Sugar	4 g
Calories from Fat 35	**Sodium**	180 mg	**Protein**	10 g
% Daily Value Vitamin A 10%	Vitamin C 20%	Calcium 4%	Iron 15%	

Lemon Garlic Halibut

Serves 6
Serving size: 3½ oz (100 g)

1 tsp (5 mL) olive oil
1 tsp (5 mL) butter
1 cup (250 mL) thinly sliced fresh mushrooms
¼ cup (50 mL) chopped green onions
1 tbsp (15 mL) chopped garlic
1 lb (455 g) halibut, cut into thin strips
½ cup (125 mL) low sodium chicken broth
¼ cup (50 mL) fresh lemon juice

Directions:

1. In a large skillet heat oil and butter.
2. Add mushrooms, green onions, and garlic. Cook and stir until tender and liquid is almost evaporated, about 5 minutes.
3. Add halibut; cover and cook until fish is almost cooked through, about 5 minutes.
4. Stir in chicken broth and lemon juice; cover and cook another 3 minutes.

Nutrition Facts	Amount		Amount	
Serves 6	**Fat**	3.5 g	**Carbohydrate**	2 g
Serving size 3½ oz (100 g)	Saturated Fat	1 g	Fiber	0 g
Calories 110	**Cholesterol**	25 mg	Sugar	1 g
Calories from Fat 30	**Sodium**	55 mg	**Protein**	17 g

% Daily Value   Vitamin A 4%   Vitamin C 10%   Calcium 4%   Iron   4%

Mexiloaf

Serves 8
Serving size: 3 oz (85 g)

1 large onion, minced
½ lb (225 g) ground turkey breast
½ lb (225 g) lean ground beef
1 large egg
2 tbsp (30 mL) chopped fresh cilantro
1 tsp (5 mL) dried oregano
½ tsp (2 mL) cumin powder
1 tsp (5 mL) garlic powder
2 tsp (10 mL) chili powder
½ cup (125 mL) plain bread crumbs
¼ tsp (1 mL) salt
1 cup (250 mL) low sodium chicken broth

Directions:
1. Preheat oven to 375°F (190°C).
2. In a small nonstick sauté pan, sauté onion until clear and golden.
3. Place remaining ingredients into a large mixing bowl and thoroughly combine.
4. Shape meat mixture and place into a medium size loaf pan.
5. Bake 45 minutes or until done. Internal temperature needs to reach 165°F (75°C).
6. Cut into 8 equal pieces and serve.

Nutrition Facts	Amount		Amount	
Serves 8	Fat	4.5 g	Carbohydrate	8 g
Serving size 3 oz (85 g)	Saturated Fat	1.5 g	Fiber	1 g
Calories 130	**Cholesterol**	50 mg	Sugar	2 g
Calories from Fat 40	**Sodium**	190 mg	**Protein**	15 g
% Daily Value Vitamin A 6%	Vitamin C 4%	Calcium 2%	Iron 10%	

Romano Baked Dover Sole

Servings 6
Serving size: 3-oz (85 g)

3 large eggs
¼ tsp (1 mL) garlic powder
⅛ tsp pepper
1 lb (455 g) fresh Dover sole, cut into 6 equal pieces
½ cup (125 mL) dried, grated Romano cheese
2 tsp (10 mL) butter

Directions:
1. Preheat oven to 450°F (200°C).
2. Combine eggs, garlic powder, and pepper in a shallow bowl and mix well.
3. Dredge fish in egg mixture.
4. Coat fish on both sides with Romano cheese.
5. Grease an 8-inch x 8-inch baking dish with butter and place coated fish into dish.
6. Bake 8 to 10 minutes, or until fish flakes easily when tested with a fork.

Nutrition Facts	Amount		Amount	
Serves 6	**Fat**	6 g	**Carbohydrate**	0 g
Serving size 3 oz (85 g)	Saturated Fat	3 g	Fiber	0 g
Calories 140	**Cholesterol**	85 mg	Sugar	0 g
Calories from Fat 60	**Sodium**	260 mg	**Protein**	19 g

% Daily Value   Vitamin A 4%   Vitamin C 2%   Calcium 15%   Iron 4%

Sautéed Shrimp with Lime Butter Sauce

Serves 6
Serving size: ½ cup (125 mL)

¼ cup (50 mL) dry white wine
¼ cup (50 mL) minced shallots
2 tbsp (30 mL) fresh lime juice
1 tbsp (30 mL) peeled and grated fresh ginger
2 tbsp (30 mL) fat free half and half
1 tbsp (15 mL) butter, cut into small pieces
1 plum tomato, seeded and chopped
2 tbsp (30 mL) chopped fresh cilantro
¼ tsp (1 mL) salt
⅛ tsp pepper
1 lb (455 g) raw small bay shrimp

Directions:

1. In a medium skillet combine wine, shallots, lime juice, and ginger; bring to a boil.
2. Drain mixture through a fine sieve into a bowl, reserving liquid and discarding solids.
3. Return wine liquid to skillet. Add fat free half-and-half; cook over medium heat 1 minute.
4. Add butter and stir until butter melts. Stir in tomato, cilantro, salt, and pepper.
5. Heat another large skillet coated with cooking spray over medium high heat.
6. Add shrimp and sauté for 2 minutes or until shrimp just turns pink.
7. Add shrimp to sauce mixture; toss gently to combine.

Nutrition Facts	Amount		Amount	
Serves 6	Fat	3 g	Carbohydrate	4 g
Serving size ½ cup (125 mL)	Saturated Fat	1.5 g	Fiber	0 g
Calories 120	**Cholesterol**	120 mg	Sugar	1 g
Calories from Fat 30	**Sodium**	230 mg	**Protein**	16 g
% Daily Value Vitamin A 8%	Vitamin C 8%	Calcium 6%	Iron 10%	

Sesame Salmon Stir-Fry

Serves 6
Serving size: ¾ cup (175 mL)

1 lb (455 g) fresh salmon, cut into thin strips
¼ cup (50 mL) teriyaki sauce
2 tsp (10 mL) sesame oil
1 tsp (5 mL) ground ginger
1 tsp (5 mL) garlic powder
Pepper, to taste
½ cup (125 mL) shredded carrot
½ cup (125 mL) julienned onion
½ cup (125 mL) thinly sliced zucchini

Directions:
1. Place salmon, teriyaki sauce, sesame oil, ginger, garlic, and pepper into a resealable plastic bag.
2. Let marinate for 30 minutes.
3. Heat a large sauté pan over high heat.
4. When sauté pan is hot, add salmon, and discard marinade.
5. Sauté salmon for 4 minutes turning every minute.
6. Add veggies and sauté for 5 minutes or until salmon is done.

Nutrition Facts	Amount		Amount	
Serves 6	Fat	11 g	Carbohydrate	4 g
Serving size ¾ cup (175 mL)	Saturated Fat	2.5 g	Fiber	1 g
Calories 180	**Cholesterol**	40 mg	Sugar	2 g
Calories from Fat 100	**Sodium**	140 mg	**Protein**	16 g

% Daily Value   Vitamin A 35%   Vitamin C 10%   Calcium 2%   Iron 2%

Skillet Chicken and Vegetables in Gravy

Serves 8
Serving size: ½ cup (125 mL)

1 lb (455) ground chicken breast
½ cup (125 mL) chopped onion
One 0.87-oz packet (25 g) dry turkey gravy mix
1 cup (250 mL) cold water
1 cup (250 mL) shredded carrots
1 cup (250 mL) potato, peeled, cooked and chopped
1 tsp (5 mL) dried oregano
¼ tsp (1 mL) pepper

Directions:

1. In a large skillet cook and stir the chicken and onion until the chicken is brown.
2. Whisk the gravy mix into the cold water whisking until no lumps remain. Add to chicken.
3. Stir in remaining ingredients.
4. Heat the mixture to boiling, and then reduce the heat and simmer, uncovered, stirring occasionally, about 10 minutes.

Nutrition Facts	Amount		Amount	
Serves 8	**Fat**	2 g	**Carbohydrate**	10 g
Serving size ½ cup (125 mL)	Saturated Fat	0.5 g	Fiber	1 g
Calories 120	**Cholesterol**	35 mg	Sugar	2 g
Calories from Fat 15	**Sodium**	360 mg	**Protein**	14 g
% Daily Value	Vitamin A 45%	Vitamin C 6%	Calcium 2%	Iron 4%

Southwestern Turkey Chowder

Serves 12
Serving size: 1 cup (250 mL)

1 tbsp (15 mL) canola oil
1 cup (250 mL) diced carrot
1 cup (250 mL) diced onion
1 whole jalapeno pepper, seeded and diced
1 tsp (5 mL) cumin powder
3 cloves garlic, minced
4 cups (1 L) low sodium chicken broth
2 cups (500 mL) peeled and diced potatoes

1 lb (455 g) diced, boneless, skinless turkey breast
⅓ cup (75 mL) all-purpose flour
2 ½ cups (625 mL) fat free half-and-half
1 tsp (5 mL) liquid smoke
½ cup (125 mL) grated smoked Gouda cheese
½ cup (125 mL) grated Monterey Jack cheese

Directions:

1. In a medium stockpot, heat oil over medium. Add carrot, onion, jalapenos, cumin, and garlic.
2. Stir and let brown. Pour the chicken broth into the pot; deglaze the pot.
3. Add the potatoes and bring to a boil. Cover and simmer 15 minutes or until potatoes are tender.
4. Add the turkey; bring back to a simmer. Cover and cook for 10 minutes.
5. Combine the flour and the fat free half-and-half and mix until mostly smooth; add to chowder and stir until thickened.
6. Turn chowder to low heat; lightly simmer for 20 minutes.
7. Remove from heat and add liquid smoke and cheeses; mix in.

Nutrition Facts	Amount		Amount	
Serves 12	**Fat**	4.5 g	**Carbohydrate**	16 g
Serving size 1 cup (250 mL)	Saturated Fat	1.5 g	Fiber	1 g
Calories 170	**Cholesterol**	20 mg	Sugar	5 g
Calories from Fat 40	**Sodium**	170 mg	**Protein**	16 g
% Daily Value Vitamin A 40%	Vitamin C 10%	Calcium 15%	Iron 6%	

Teriyaki Turkey Burger

Serves 4
Serving size: 1 patty (115 g)

1 lb (455 g) ground turkey breast
1 tsp (5 mL) fresh finely chopped ginger root
2 tsp (10 mL) chopped fresh garlic
1 tsp (5 mL) sesame oil
½ cup (125 mL) chopped fresh mushrooms
1 tsp (5 mL) onion powder
¼ tsp (1 mL) pepper
1 tbsp (15 mL) low sodium soy sauce

Directions:
1. Preheat oven to 350°F (180°C).
2. Place all ingredients into a medium bowl and mix until combined. Form into 4 equal patties.
3. Spray a rimmed baking sheet with nonstick cooking spray. Place patties on the baking sheet and bake for 15 minutes, turning halfway through, or until internal temperature reaches 165°F (75°C).

Nutrition Facts	Amount		Amount	
Serves 4	**Fat**	3 g	**Carbohydrate**	2 g
Serving size 1 patty (115 g)	Saturated Fat	0 g	Fiber	0 g
Calories 140	**Cholesterol**	45 mg	Sugar	0 g
Calories from Fat 25	**Sodium**	200 mg	**Protein**	29 g

% Daily Value   Vitamin A 0%   Vitamin C 0%   Calcium 0%   Iron 10%

Tuscan Caper Crab

Serves 6
Serving size: ½ cup (125 mL)

2 tsp (10 mL) olive oil
1 tsp (5 mL) fresh garlic, chopped
1 tbsp (15 mL) capers, drained
2 green onions, chopped
½ large green bell pepper, finely chopped
½ cup (125 mL) diced fresh tomato
1 lb (455 g) fresh crabmeat, removed from shell
1 tbsp (15 mL) chopped fresh basil
1 tsp (5 mL) chopped fresh oregano
¼ cup (50 mL) fresh lemon juice

Directions:

1. In a large sauté pan over medium-high heat, add oil.
2. When oil is hot, add garlic, capers, and green onions. Sauté for 3 minutes.
3. Add green bell pepper and tomatoes. Sauté for 5 minutes.
4. Add crab, fresh herbs, and lemon juice. Sauté for 3 minutes.

Nutrition Facts		Amount		Amount	
Serves 6		**Fat**	2.5 g	**Carbohydrate**	4 g
Serving size ½ cup (125 mL)		Saturated Fat	0 g	Fiber	1 g
Calories 110		**Cholesterol**	55 mg	Sugar	1 g
Calories from Fat 25		**Sodium**	330 mg	**Protein**	17 g

% Daily Value   Vitamin A 6%   Vitamin C 35%   Calcium 6%   Iron 4%

Conclusion

Weight loss surgery is life changing. You will be faced with old habits and new challenges throughout your journey. Setting yourself up for success at the beginning will make it easier to stick to your plan and reach your goals. Part of that plan includes new foods and new methods of food preparation.

Recipes for Weight Loss Surgery Success is intended to help you through the first weeks and months after your surgery, but these recipes may be used for a lifetime simply because you enjoy them. Sometimes you may not feel well and just want easy-to-prepare foods. If you have an adjustable gastric band, it is recommended that you eat smooth foods and then soft foods for several days after a fill or adjustment to your band. For whatever your reason, keep this book handy.

Make a commitment to stick to the tried and true rules as you move to eating regular foods for the rest of your healthier life.

Rules for Long-term Success:

1. **Eat only at planned mealtimes.** *No* grazing. Grazing leads to overeating and weight regain.
2. **Chew, chew, chew, and eat slowly, approximately 20 to 30 minutes per meal.** Take small bites and chew each bite at least 20 to 30 times. The more you chew the more your teeth will break down the food, and the food will be less likely to get stuck. Giving yourself time to eat is imperative to making sure

you're not overfilling your pouch or getting food stuck from taking bites that are too big.

3. **Do not overeat.** Pay attention to your portion sizes. It is always good to have a scale and measuring cups and measuring spoons on hand to keep your portions to the recommended amounts. Remember, as hard as it may seem, it's okay to leave food on your plate if you feel full. Most people report a feeling of pressure as they begin to feel full.

4. **Do not eat and drink at the same time.** Consuming food and drinking liquids at the same time can give you a false feeling of being full when in fact it's just liquids. The liquids can also flush the food from your pouch and cause you to be hungry between meals. The worst-case scenario is consuming both foods and liquids together, which can cause you to regurgitate.

5. **Eat high quality, nutrient-dense foods.** Include adequate protein to meet your goal, fruits, vegetables, and whole grains. As a rule, avoid processed foods that are salty, crunchy, and sweet. Fresh is best!

6. **Stay hydrated.** Drink a minimum of 64 fluid ounces (2 L) of water or other low-calorie beverages per day.

7. **Take your supplements daily.** Follow the recommendations from your doctor or dietitian. Not taking your supplements as prescribed can lead to serious vitamin and/or mineral deficiencies.

8. **Be active.** Work toward 30 to 60 minutes of physical activity most days of the week. It will help you lose weight and physical activity is critical to maintaining weight loss.

9. **Follow up with your doctor.** Follow-ups are a lifetime commitment. Always keep your appointments and get your blood work done as ordered.

10. **Attend a support group or use online support.** These are great ways to stay in contact with other folks who have also gone through the same weight loss surgery as you have. If you need a hand, someone is there to help, and you in turn, can help others.

It's important to remember where you came from and have a goal to work toward. When you get discouraged, remember your motivation for having weight loss surgery. Staying committed to your goal may seem tough, but look ahead and remind yourself of the benefits of weight loss. The worst thing that can happen once you've made this commitment is you will be left with a healthy new you!

This book is to be used as a general guideline and in no way replaces any information your doctor or dietitian has given you. Although we can assure that we follow the guidelines of the American Society for Metabolic and Bariatric Surgery and the American Dietetic Association, surgical practices differ their recommendations based on your personal needs and goals.

We wish you success in your healthier new life.

Cook Smart   Eat Smart . . .
Chef Dave Fouts   Vicki Bovee, MS, RD, LD

Common Measurement Abbreviations

Abbreviation	Measure
C, c	Cup
fl oz	Fluid ounce
gal	Gallon
g	Gram
kg	Kilogram
L, l	Liter
lb	Pound
mL, ml	Milliliter
oz	Ounce
pt	Pint
qt	Quart
t, tsp	Teaspoon
T, TB, tbsp	Tablespoon

Cooking Measures

Measurement	US Measure	Metric Measure
Dash	Less than ⅛ teaspoon	—
3 teaspoons	1 tablespoon	15 milliliters
1 cup	16 tablespoons	250 milliliters
2 cups	1 pint	500 milliliters
2 pints	1 quart	1 liter
4 quarts	1 gallon	4 liters
16 ounces	1 pound	455 grams

Measurement Conversion Charts

Volume Measures

US Measure	Fluid Ounces	Metric Measure
¼ teaspoon	—	1 milliliter
½ teaspoon	—	2 milliliter
¾ teaspoon	—	3 milliliter
1 teaspoon	1/6	5 milliliter
1 tablespoon	½	15 milliliter
¼ cup	2	50 milliliter
⅓ cup	2.5	75 milliliter
½ cup	4	120 milliliter
⅔ cup	5	150 milliliter
¾ cup	6	175 milliliter
1 cup	8	250 milliliter
1 pint	16	500 milliliter
1 quart	32	1 liter
1 gallon	128	4 liters

Weight Measures

US Measure	Metric Measure
1 ounce	30 grams
2 ounces	55 grams
3 ounces	85 grams
4 ounces	115 grams
8 ounces	225 grams
16 ounces	455 grams
2.2 pounds	1 kilogram

Index

About the Authors

Chef Dave Fouts, "The World's First Bariatric Chef" and clinical dietitian, Vicki Bovee, MS, RD, LD, founded Simply Smart Food, a culinary and nutrition company specializing in weight management and bariatric, weight loss surgery, services and programs, in 2007. They have worked with major companies such as Allergan Canada, Obesity Help, JourneyLite, Kellogg's, and PepsiCo. Both are Advisory Board members for WLS Lifestyles and Obesity Action Coalition.

Chef Dave Fouts received his culinary degree in 1994 from the Florida Culinary Institute. In 2002 Chef Dave had weight loss surgery and is maintaining a 270 pound weight loss. These days you can find him performing at cooking seminars across the country, writing for bariatric publications and his website, www.chefdave.org. Chef Dave lives in Edmond, Oklahoma.

Vicki is a registered dietitian with over 25 years experience in weight management, specializing in bariatric nutrition since 2003. In addition to working with Chef Dave, she works with weight loss surgery patients before and after surgery, conducting classes and individual counseling sessions and developing patient education materials. She is a member of the American Dietetic Association, American Society of Metabolic and Bariatric Surgery, and Obesity Action Coalition. Vicki received a M.S. degree from Montana State University and a B.S. degree from the University of Wisconsin- Stevens Point. Vicki lives in West Vancouver, British Columbia.